everything is NORMAL until proven otherwise

A Book About Wraparound Services

KARL W. DENNIS and IRA S. LOURIE

CWLA Press • Washington, DC

CWLA Press is an imprint of the Child Welfare League of America. The Child Welfare League of America is the nation's oldest and largest membership-based child welfare organization. We are committed to engaging people everywhere in promoting the well-being of children, youth, and their families, and protecting every child from harm. All proceeds from the sale of this book support CWLA's programs in behalf of children and families.

CHILD WELFARE LEAGUE OF AMERICA, INC.
Washington, DC
E-mail: books@cwla.org

CURRENT PRINTING (last digit)
10 9 8

Cover and text design by Jennifer R. Geanakos
Edited by Tegan A. Culler

Printed in the United States of America

ISBN: 978-1-58760-078-4

Library of Congress Cataloging-in-Publication Data
Dennis, Karl W.
  Everything is normal until proven otherwise: a book about wraparound services /
Karl W. Dennis and Ira S. Lourie.
      p. cm.
  Summary: "Through personal stories and commentary by two of the model's creators, this book describes the evolution and philosophy behind Wraparound, a model of individualized service provision for children and families in the social service system"—
Provided by publisher.
  ISBN: 978-1-58760-078-4 (pbk. : alk. paper)
  1. Psychiatric social work—United States. 2. Mentally ill children—Family relationships.
  3. Social work with children with mental disabilities—United States. I. Lourie, Ira S.
II. Title.

HV690.U6D46 2006
362.2083—dc22   2005037061

The writing of this book was supported by a grant from the Annie E. Casey Foundation. Its publishing is being supported by another grant from the Annie E. Casey Foundation and a subsidy from the Child and Family Branch of the Center for Mental Health Services, Substance Abuse and Mental Health Administration, Department of Health and Human Services.

The authors will donate a substantial portion of their proceeds from the sales of this book to agencies and organizations that provide services and advocacy for children and their families.

The stories in this book are based on the experiences of the authors working with children and adolescents and their families, through the Chicago-area service agency, Kaleidescope. In the majority of the stories, the names of the people and some of their identifying characteristics have been changed to respect the confidentiality of those individuals and families. In one case, an individual who has worked with Karl at Kaleidoscope has agreed to have his real name published in this book.

This book is dedicated to all those children, youth, and families who have taught us about their struggles and helped us understand the best ways to support them.

"The plural of anecdote is policy."

—Dan Fox

contents

foreword

by Gary Blau, PhD

Branch Chief, Child and Family Branch,
SAMHSA Center for Mental Health Services,

Everything Is Normal Until Proven Otherwise offers the most eloquent understanding of the Wraparound process written to date. More than that, this book provides a rare and delightful glimpse into a partnership between Karl Dennis and Ira Lourie. Karl is a child welfare administrator firmly rooted in the solid foundation of a strengths-based, family-driven community perspective. He and his partners at Kaleidoscope have spent the past 30 years refining service-delivery strategies based on the insight and wisdom of the youth and families with whom they have had the honor of working. Ira Lourie, a noted psychiatrist and self-described federal bureaucrat, was instrumental in implementing the Child and Adolescent Service System Program (CASSP) out of what is now the Center for Mental Health Services in the mid-1980s. During his tenure at the Center for Mental Health Services Ira established the foundation for developing systems of care and set a high standard of excellence for states, tribes, territories and communities working to identify and implement new strategies to improve children's mental health services.

Karl is a master storyteller who uses his own experience and the experiences of the many youth and families who have touched his life to help educate communities about the Wraparound process both in America and internationally. Karl's vivid stories quickly immerse the reader in the simplistic elegance of the Wraparound process, rendering you intimately familiar with the youth and families who were engaged with Karl and Kaleidoscope. Complementing Karl's stories is Ira's insightful analysis, which expertly frames the stories within the context of the basic elements of individualized, or Wraparound, service approaches.

Each story in this book underscores central tenets of the Wraparound approach. When you finish this book, you will come away with an understanding of Wraparound that is embedded in the rich context of family and community. As Karl says in the book, "just let yourself get the feel of it." If you heed his advice, you will understand that Wraparound is not a 'thing' or 'product,' but a process with unique surprises and joys brought forth by families and providers who are connected with each other, sharing the common goal of making life better for youth and families.

Another equally important, though somewhat subtle, message in *Everything is Normal Until Proven Otherwise* is that it provides a unique window from which to view the cultivation of a relationship and partnership between Karl Dennis and Ira Lourie—and the greater partnership of community and federal government that is represented by their relationship. In the early 1980s, Karl and his colleagues in the community of Chicago were determined to make systemic changes in how children with severe challenges and their families were served. At the same time, Ira Lourie and his colleagues at the federal level were determined to provide funding and a structure within which to study and replicate examples of excellence in improving services for children and families.

The partnership that resulted and flourished is exactly the type of partnership called for today in the recent President's New Freedom Commission on Mental Health report, *Achieving the Promise: Transforming Mental Health Care in America* (SAMHSA, 2003). The Substance Abuse and Mental Health Services Administration (SAMHSA) that houses the Child, Adolescent, and Family Branch, of which Ira Lourie is the former head, has accepted the challenge to transform mental health in America. The story of Kaleidoscope, Wraparound, Karl Dennis and Ira Lourie serves as an important example of the transformation process in action. Their willingness to constructively challenge accepted practices of the day, to really listen to youth and families to help identify a better way to provide services, and to evaluate and learn from their efforts, serve as an important reminder and benchmark for our current efforts to transform mental health services in America. The collaborative spirit between federal government and local community, described so well in this excellent book, must be nurtured and developed if we are to truly transform mental health in America. If ever there was a model for transformation, Karl and Ira are again leading the way.

Initially nurtured with Ira Lourie's guidance, the Child, Adolescent, and Family Branch has grown significantly. The nation owes a great debt of gratitude to Ira for his steadfast commitment to improving services for children and families. Equally important was his willingness to recognize challenges, listen to families and providers in the trenches, and make changes accordingly.

The nation also owes a great debt of gratitude to Karl Dennis. Karl has been a tireless advocate for promoting a more humanistic, strengths-based approach to help youth and families achieve a level of balance that offers them the opportunity to be together. As Karl notes in this book, "if for some strange reason young people were fortunate enough to run away from the institution, they all ran in the same direction–they all ran home." His great body of work over the past 30 years has been focused on identifying ways to make "home" a healthy place.

Everything is Normal Until Proven Otherwise is a celebration. The book celebrates a genuine way of listening to the needs of youth and families, and it honors the courage of people, who, in the mid-70s, were convinced they could do it better than their supervisors and administrators (and they were right!). Finally, it pays tribute to the steadfast commitment of a noted psychiatrist in a key position in federal government with the foresight and wisdom to advocate for funding efforts to strengthen children's mental health services across America, and a man who turned these funds into action.

Take your time reading this book. Savor each chapter. Let the voices of the youth and families' stories surround you so that you can truly experience the Wraparound process as it was meant to be.

foreword

by Patrick McCarthy

Vice President, System and Service Reform
Annie E. Casey Foundation

You're in for a treat. It's not often that the theory and practice of helping troubled kids and their families is explained clearly and powerfully, through engaging, accessible, and illuminating stories of real lives and real help. This book goes well beyond that standard by bringing concepts and ideas to life through the stories of real people.

The source of this success is a excellent marriage of talents. Karl Dennis and Ira Lourie are both gifted, and they've managed to combine their gifts to create a wonderful book.

Karl is a connector: he connects to people with the kind of care and attention that is profoundly transformative, and he connects people to other people through a healing belief in kids and a deep faith in the power of families. He channels this belief and faith through a heavy dose of hard-earned wisdom and common sense. He helps all of us to find our own belief and faith in the deep urge to change things for the better: children, families, teachers, helpers, his own staff, and the field at large.

Karl is also a teller of tales, stories that pull us in, challenging our conventional wisdom, and forcing us to stretch to think out of our boxed-in frames. He uses his story-gift strategically, to open us up to the possible and to convince us that the improbable is really just around a slight bend from everyday experience, if we're willing to go along for the ride. I've heard almost all of these stories before, while sitting in a variety of rapt audiences hanging on every word. And almost every time, the response is the same. You can almost hear a wave of people responding internally with a kind of quiet, thoughtful, "Huh? How about that? Could that really work? Could I do that?"

Ira is an innovator, a systems genius, and an organizer of ideas. Twenty-five years ago, when he and Karl inspired each other along with so many others in the field, Ira had a platform as the highest official in the Federal government concerned with mental health services for children. Working with Karl and many other leaders in the field, Ira brought the long-neglected needs of children to the forefront of mental health planning and programming in this country. The work that is his legacy continues to grow and thrive.

Drawing on his talent for analysis and synthesis, Ira pulls the theory and practice ideas from Karl's stories. His insights add the "Aha!" moment to the "Huh?" moment. They make you want to re-read the stories, and they help uncover the driving themes and critical ideas behind them.

The Annie E. Casey Foundation felt that Karl's stories were a national treasure that needed to be in print, and we gave a grant to Karl and Ira to write them into a book. This is the result; a book you will dog-ear and keep close whether you're a parent, a teen, a scholar, a helper, or a policymaker. Indeed, you're in for a treat, but turn the page knowing that you run the risk of seeing the world differently by the time you're through reading.

acknowledgements and about this book

We would like to acknowledge the many people who helped us in the writing of this book. First, the book would not exist if not for the foresight and generosity of the Annie E. Casey Foundation, which initially gave us a grant to support the writing of the book, and later gave a second grant to subsidize part of its publication. The foundation's Patrick McCarthy, Mareasa Isaacs, and Doug Nelson are all deserving of our gratitude. Secondly, the Center for Mental Health Services of the Substance Abuse and Mental Health Services Administration has also partly subsidized the book's publication, and we would like to thank Gary Blau and Sybil Goldman for their support. We are both grateful and honored that Dixie Jordan agreed to contribute an introductory essay for the book on the role of families in the care of their children; it sets the perfect tone for the messages we have tried to get across. Barbara Sample, director of the Montana Family Support Network and a former English professor, edited the draft as a contribution to the book. We thank her not only for this valuable contribution, but for her ongoing support of our efforts, especially her encouragement to complete the book through praise of our early chapters, in spite of her heavy editing. We'd also like to acknowledge our editor at CWLA Press, Tegan Culler, for organizing the beginning of the book and for her work on the subsequent chapters. We are indebted to Barbara Huff, former Executive Director of the Federation of Families for Child Mental Health, for her comments and support in writing the chapter concerning families. We would especially like to thank the children, families, and workers at Kaleidoscope, particularly Olivia DelGiudice, who was Karl's second-in-command for many years. Finally, three special people helped us conceptualize, write, and rewrite the drafts of the book and without whose support it would never have been completed: Kathy Dennis, Bonnie Lourie Smith, and Carrol Lourie.

In *Everything Is Normal Until Proven Otherwise,* we hope to help the reader understand how we came to appreciate Wraparound. Much of the book focuses on the principles of delivering Wraparound services, and most chapters begin with a story or several stories that Karl has told about his experience at Kaleidoscope, the agency in Chicago he directed for more than 20 years, and finish with commentary by Ira on the story and that particular principle of Wraparound. Karl's stories are printed in this font; Ira's commentary in this font.

Three of the chapters are exceptions. In the first chapter, we present Karl's story about the evolution of Kaleidoscope and its form of Wraparound, which the organization called Individualized Services. This story is presented without Ira's commentary. In the next-to-last chapter, Ira tells of his personal introduction to the principles of Wraparound; that chapter is called "Everything is Normal Until Proven Otherwise," a phrase that became the title of this book. In the last chapter, Karl finishes the book with a summary of his feelings about Wraparound. In addition, we have also included an epilogue in which we offer follow-up on as many of the people in the stories as possible.

Karl, a social worker by nature, began his career in the streets with young people who were having problems adjusting to their worlds. Ira is a child psychiatrist by training who is grounded within the context of psychoanalytic theory and who began his career as a federal bureaucrat. Somehow the two of us got together, but, before that time, we independently came to similar conclusions about how to intervene with children, adolescents, and their parents who have unique and overwhelming problems. At Kaleidoscope, Karl's version of this thought became the underpinnings of Wraparound. At the federal government level, Ira applied this thinking to the development of services for adolescents who had run away or who had been victims of child abuse and neglect. Karl and Ira first met in 1977, when Karl invited Ira to speak about abused and neglected adolescents at a conference in Chicago that Kaleidoscope had helped to plan. We were instantly compatible in our views. We did not get together again until nine years later, however, when Karl was invited to introduce Wraparound to a group that Ira had brought together for the federal

Child and Adolescent Service System Program, known as CASSP. We quickly realized that our thinking, which had been so compatible in 1977, had matured sufficiently by 1986 that we had each created a program—a clinical one and a service delivery one—based on those same principles. Wraparound then went on to become the expression of case-level service delivery within the CASSP program as CASSP attempted to change the way services were delivered by states and communities.

Interestingly, the term "Wraparound" did not come from either of us. You can read Kaleidoscope's staff training manuals and you'll never see it there. Our friend and colleague, Lenore Behar, created it in her work in North Carolina. At the same time we were working in Chicago and Washington, DC, Lenore was in North Carolina developing a program for some of that state's hardest-to-serve youngsters, on whose behalf a class action suit had been brought. The program she created was known as the Willie M. Program, and was developed to serve youth who were retarded, mentally ill, and aggressive—in a community-based setting. She believed these youngsters could be served in the community rather than in institutions, if you "wrapped" services around them instead of walls. Thus, the term Wraparound services evolved.

Finally, most of the stories told in this book come from the period when Karl worked at Kaleidoscope, and as a result, they sometimes contain references to Kaleidoscope in the present tense, which we did not always change.

—Karl W. Dennis and Ira S. Lourie

introduction

Walking the Circle:
The Changed Perceptions Required for Wraparound

by Dixie Jordan

*While we can listen to the stories of others and they can
listen to ours, perhaps the most healing feature is that
we, the storyteller, get to hear our own story.*

—Charles Whitfield

It has been said that some things are best explored from a distance, and that time heals all. Interesting that as I sit here remembering the first time that my son was diagnosed with depression, anxiety, and attention deficit/ hyperactivity disorder, that the weight of that moment comes back with an acuity barely diminished by two intervening decades. What I remember is the unspoken accusation and implied responsibility that came with the diagnoses and that hung, almost visibly, in the air before settling across my shoulders like a mantle of lead.

The clinician who had completed the diagnostic profile of my son was kind enough, but, well, clinical. She did her best to secure a commitment from me that our family would participate in a therapeutic recovery process, but did not even think to ask the questions, "Do you have other children and how are they? What do you think we should do? What is your son really good at? What are some of the things you do to support your child emotionally? How can we work together?" Instead, she recommended parenting classes, asked how often my husband and I argued and about what, what other family "problems" existed, and wondered aloud why it was that a 9-year-old might appear depressed. Noting that I am Native American, she even asked if I drank while pregnant!

As wisdom keeper for my family, narrator of our family history, scientist with a record of family interventions and outcomes, and therapist for the countless wounds of childhood experienced by both my children, it really hurt that I was not consulted about the area in which I possessed the greatest expertise—my own child. On that day, I became the origin of the problem, not the knowledgeable collaborator. I never called that therapist again, and I'm quite sure that as a result I became diagnosed as "resistant to treatment, in denial, and overprotective." The feelings of despair, humiliation, and deep anger I experienced reminded me of another event that happened when I was just 5 years old.

My parents had driven me to the physician's office for the smallpox vaccination required to enter school. Once in the office, I bolted and ran for the door, but was cornered in the nurse's chamber, dragged back into the office, and over my vehement objections, vaccinated. I was furious. The loss of power was humiliating, and I decided on the spot to run away as soon as I could get home and pack.

My grandfather was waiting at our house when we returned from the doctor, with his fishing rod and an invitation to catch some fish. Still smarting, I told him my story. He agreed that running away was an option, but one that we could perhaps think about while fishing.

As we sat in the boat, Grandpa asked if I knew why a vaccination was needed. I said yes, but that I had a right to get sick if I wanted to, and that the vaccination should have been my choice. He agreed. He quietly pointed out, during the course of the afternoon, that should I become ill by not having a vaccination, I would also infect my younger brothers and sisters. In my family of thirteen children, caring for the young was the responsibility of all the older family members. Endangering younger siblings through a lack of personal responsibility was out of the question! How I wish that my parents had thought to talk to me about these things before taking me for the vaccination, then asking what I wanted to do while explaining the nature and consequences of my choice.

What I have learned over the years as a parent of two now-adult children and as an advocate for families is that listening and sharing the wisdom that each of us possesses, and reserving judgment about the knowledge of others, is fundamental to the health of children and families—and to their communities. Families, however they define themselves, learn from their members and from other families how to obtain services, care for their children, manage their households and fit into the fabric of their community.

It is so easy to lose sight of the strengths and power of families of children experiencing emotional distress when there is so much pain and chaos! It is so easy to use parental inadequacy as the explanation for that which we do not thoroughly understand. It is so easy to develop a litany of things gone wrong and a prescription for their correction. It is so easy to blame families themselves, however subtly, for the challenges they experience.

When I was 9, my Grandpa and I beached our fishing boat on a broad sandbar to wait out an impending rain. As we waited, he found a stick on the beach, and drew a circle in the sand about fourteen feet in diameter. He asked me to lie on my side in the sand at the top of the circle, close one eye and scan the circle with the other, and then say what the object was that he was placing in its center. I saw what I knew surely to be the broad end of a pinecone, round, brown, about four inches wide, and with a small stem. I did not ask if I was correct, I simply announced that I was looking at the end of a pinecone.

Without responding, Grandpa then covered the object with his hand and asked me to move to another position on the circle, ninety degrees from the first, and to take another look. When he removed his hand, something wafer-thin was in the center of the circle, with a twig protruding. Grandpa had found a large rusty washer on the beach and inserted a twig in its small center hole. He knew that I would make an assumption about what I saw, based on my own limited experience. He then taught me that it was often necessary to consider a different perspective.

When my eldest child was young, even strangers would comment on what a good mother I must be to have such a well-behaved and compliant child. I enjoyed those early accolades and truly believed that those parents whose children were generally demolishing the environments around them were simply not very skilled in childrearing. Both my perspective and my experience were limited in those days. How I wish that I could personally apologize to all those parents who were the recipients of my reproachful glances in my "good mother" stage of development!

Most adults in the world today are parents, and the majority of us have children who do not have mental health concerns. Everything in our experience suggests that when our children are successful and obedient, it is because of good parenting. We are reinforced socially for having well-behaved children from friends, grandparents, and even from strangers. It makes sense, from this perspective, to attribute undesirable behaviors in children to the failure of their parents to provide appropriate guidance or to set firm limits.

When children have emotional problems, their behaviors can cut their parents off from the supports of others. As a result, they often forget that they are skillful, intelligent beings and yield their personal power to the experts that stream in and out of their lives. This is never without consequence, often in the form of an abundance of well-disguised (or ill-disguised) resentment, or worse, a fatalistic acceptance of services that we know are simply time wasters or a refusal of services altogether. We give up on ourselves as competent beings, and begin to paint a new picture of ourselves as inadequate or incompetent, which then compels us to maintain integrity by becoming inadequate or incompetent. That is why the "family story" is so important!

A family story is a shared learning experience. It requires a Teller and a Listener, a very safe environment, and an understanding that each teller relates his or her story as it is remembered, either positively or negatively. Family members will each have a story, and each is valid from the perspective of the teller. Stories are not just statements of fact; they convey the teller's perspective, expectations, skills, judgments, and feelings. Stories transmit all kinds of knowledge, when the listener has the capacity to hear themes and translates the themes into supports and services. Listening to the family story requires respecting the story as the story that teaches its listeners about the core capabilities and strengths of each family. Families who share their stories with us freely bestow the cement and water for a foundation upon which friends, community members and mental health professionals can help each family to build their desired outcomes and find the supports they need to reach their outcomes.

Family stories are the underpinnings of successful Wraparound. They are an account of the developmental and event histories within families that have a direct relationship to that family's health. Telling the family story not only helps family members to organize their experience, it can also help them to think about their amazing strengths and skills. Family storytellers inherently know—or learn—to give a meaningful order to the events or circumstances in the story they are telling.

This does not mean that their stories are always, or even mostly, positive. For some families, the presence of overwhelming obstacles in all areas of their life contributes to a negative image they hold of themselves, or of their children. The professional role in the family story is not that of an expert who simply diagnoses and treats problems, but an ally who searches out the strengths and capabilities of the family through their story, and then helps them to use those strengths and capabilities to build the lives they want for themselves. As more communities and states adopt family-driven practice, it becomes the sacred responsibility—and the sacred honor—of those of us who work closely with families to find better ways to listen to the family story.

Providing services and supports to families in the Wraparound process does not diminish the knowledge of an individual but enhances the wisdom and skills of the group, in a process that is based on profound respect for families. It does demand new skills of the uninitiated, such as learning how to share power, and how to accept that families are decisionmakers when the decisions they make are not the ones we think they should make.

The stories in this gem of a book illustrate so beautifully the need for each of us to walk the circle and to take a fresh look at each family from various perspectives to discover what is right and good and working for them. Nothing in the world can take the place of one person intentionally listening to another. It may be the simplest of all interventions, but there is no doubt that it is also the most significant. Karl's sensitive stories and Ira's focus on learning opportunities that result from the stories make this an unusual and useful book on excellence in providing services to children with emotional problems and their families. They call it Wraparound. The approach they encourage relies on the strengths of children and families to define the needed help and supports. Their Wraparound truly listens to the children and families and walks us around the circle to new perspectives. When we are all able to convey to our families that they have been heard, and that we understand what it is that they are saying and will support them in its attainment, we can then truly say that we are Wraparound practitioners.

tyrone and carol

How We Started Doing this Strange Job

At Kaleidoscope, Wraparound started in the mid-1970s, at a time when the State of Illinois had about 1,000 children and adolescents in out-of-state placements. The state, on discovering that one of those children had been chained to a tree, ordered all of them back into Illinois. This was about the same time we were starting Kaleidoscope.

Now, I would love to tell you that Kaleidoscope was started by some really brilliant people who had vision and could see the future, but the reality is it was just four young men who were incredibly arrogant and were convinced they knew how to do things better than their supervisors and administrators in the institutions where they worked. Every evening after working the 3 P.M. to 11 P.M. shift, these four guys would retire to the local "library," which was really a tavern. It seemed each time they did this they would start to moan and groan about the services that were being delivered in those institutions. One night, after moaning and groaning a little more than usual, they decided what they needed to do was to start an agency of their own. An indication of how backward they were was the fact that they spent the first 45 minutes naming the agency.

Only then did it dawn on one of the guys that, if they were going to run an agency, maybe they should have a philosophy. They looked at what they had seen at the institutions they had worked in, and asked themselves what needed to change to make things work better. The first thing that occurred to them was, if for some strange reason young people were fortunate enough to run away from the institution, they all ran in the same direction—home. Regardless of what had gone on in those homes, even if the children and adolescents had been abused and neglected, they ran home like a straight shot. This realization suggested to these four young men that, possibly, some strong pull exists between children and their families, and as opposed to tearing these families apart, maybe the child-parent bond needed to be strengthened. Maybe home would be a better environment for providing services to children than moving them into residential institutions.

Then, one of the other young men started to talk about a realization that had recently come to him as a parent. You see, having just had a son three months before, he had discovered that it was important for him to commit himself to loving his child and taking care of him. He knew he would do this whether his child was blind, whether he was deaf, whether he was fat, whether he was skinny—whatever. His child was his responsibility. He asked the group, "If we are going to take the responsibility of providing care to someone else's children, shouldn't we extend to them the same commitment we extend to our own?"

They all agreed and decided this new agency would have a "No Reject" (no decline) philosophy, which stated "no matter who is referred to our agency, we will provide services for them." If their new agency didn't have a service to meet a particular child's needs, then one would be designed specifically for that child. This seemed to make a lot of sense.

Then one of these guys said, "It seems as though when young people come into institutions and don't fit in, they start to act out and break things. Then, we have a tendency to discharge them from these institutions—in other words, we kick them out!"

The group then came to the conclusion that none of them could ever conceive of throwing one of his own children out of his family, no matter what the child had done. "Maybe," they said, "we need to extend the same commitment to the people we serve?"

From this they all agreed there should also be a "No Eject" (no punitive discharge) philosophy, which meant that when a child came into their new agency, regardless of what this child did, it would not result in him or her being thrown out.

They were feeling pretty good about that. Then one of the guys said, "Hey, wait a minute! You know, not all discharges are negative. Sometimes, youth come into our institutions and do very well. We've worked with them for a year, and at the end, they don't appear to need this type of intensive service any more, so we send them to foster care or some other less intensive service. And, all of us professionals agree this makes sense, in fact everybody thinks it makes sense except the young people themselves.

"I think," he continued, "it doesn't make sense to the young people because first we ask them to develop relationships with us and their peers and to develop therapeutic relationships. Then, their reward for this is that they lose those peers, adults, and therapists and have to get new ones. And, we wonder why youth don't like therapy! If people keep being moved from system to system, and having their therapists changed frequently, then of course they're not going to be very happy about it."

So the four guys decided that rather than changing young people from system to system, they should be kept in one agency with just the services being changed to meet their needs. "As children's needs change, the same people as before will be surrounding them and taking care of them and only the services they deliver will change," went that philosophy.

Well, the next morning the guys woke up with hangovers, but they had committed themselves to providing this new special type of care. When the State of Illinois, which, you may remember, had 1,000 children and adolescents coming back from out of state, found out that some fools would be willing to provide services to anyone who was referred to them, they sent this new agency the most difficult youth. It may shock you to find out that I was not one of those four guys, but I came along shortly after. The crazy agency we started was Kaleidoscope. It took them 45 minutes to come up with the name and, after more than 30 years, I still have trouble spelling it!

At first, Kaleidoscope only ran small group homes, each one limited to five youth. These homes were always in the community and, of course, had both boys and girls in the same home. We did this because we wanted to normalize the lifestyle of those children. We understood that the normal way of life is for families not to choose the sex of their children and most families we knew had both boys and girls in them. And, we wanted to run our group homes in a similar way, so they would be as home-like as possible.

One of the things we noticed was that some of the young people who were coming back from out of state were between the ages of 17 and 21 and had been in numerous placements. They had been everywhere! One could overhear conversations between them in which a new youth would be greeted, "Hey man, didn't I meet you at the Brown School in Texas?"

"Naah, I think it was at Excelsior in Colorado," would be the reply.

These youngsters have been sent all over the country, and on coming to Kaleidoscope, they had averaged 19 previous placements. All of them had run away from at least two or three different places. At that time in history, most of them were diagnosed as "sociopaths." I like to tease clinicians by telling them how old they are by how they refer to these children. If you've been out of school 15 years or longer, you will most likely call them "sociopaths"; between 5 years and 15 years, you would probably label them "borderlines"; and if you've only been out of school 5 years or less, or you read a lot, you will say they have "conduct disorder." A friend of my tried to get a new diagnosis into the official psychiatric diagnosis manual known as DSM-IV: He thought we should refer to these young people as having "multiple placement disorder!" This is really a better description of who they are, because for some strange reason, if whatever we are doing doesn't work or doesn't work long enough, we usually come up with a diagnosis which suggests there was nothing we could have done with them in the first place. Then the children are sent somewhere else.

One of the problems that institutional programs (as well as many community-based programs) have is that they deliver only one kind of service. Therefore, when a child cannot make it in that particular service, he or she must leave. Now, it's obvious to me that you cannot run "no decline, no punitive discharge" services with only one service environment. You will notice I use the word environment as opposed to program. I hate the word program, because this term suggests something which has been set up with a certain mold, using a method of service or treatment that everyone has to fit into, whether it works for them or not. The term environment only suggests it is a place where people live. Rather than having only one or two services for a child to fit into, we felt we needed to create an individualized set of services for each child. The place they spent their time was not to be considered a program or service, but an environment within which we would deliver all needed individualized services.

As I mentioned before, many of these young people who Illinois was bringing back were from 17 to 21 years old. Even though they had histories of extreme physical and sexual aggression, suicidal behaviors, and firesetting, we decided that, since they were going to be emancipated soon anyway, we needed to force them into independence, whether or not they were ready for it. We felt they needed to be in the community rather than in institutions. Instead of surrounding them with brick and mortar, we wanted to surround them with people. The people we hire to surround those children or young adults were picked because they had a sense of humor and fit the needs, wants, and strengths of the children. When a youth was into music, we would find a person who was into music. For someone who was into mechanics, we would find a person who was into mechanics. Size often had a lot to do with it, too! (In the old days, we used to call those people "friendly gorillas!" We can't call them this anymore because we can't bill Medicaid for that service, so they are now called things like "Recreational Technicians," a service for which we can bill.)

We were not perfect, and as Kaleidoscope developed, we made mistakes. One of the first things we did wrong was to try and change youths' lifestyles by moving them into middle-class communities. What this accomplished was to make them stick out like sore thumbs. We decided this strategy was not working and reversed ourselves. Next, we moved our independent living apartments into poor communities. This didn't work any better, because the youth stuck out like sore thumbs in this setting as well. Then we hit on the perfect place. We discovered that no matter how bizarre our young people were, if we placed them around universities, they wouldn't look any more bizarre than the freshman class at that university. (I once spent three years working on a committee at Harvard, and I can tell you that none of the youth I have ever served looked as bizarre as the students at Harvard University.) From then on, we determined that our services for older adolescents were created in collegiate neighborhoods, and we would try to move those youth into independent living in those areas as soon as we possibly could.

About the same time, some state officials came to us and asked for help. As they were bringing all of the children back from out-of-state facilities, there were not enough community-based placements for all of them, and the state had been forced to send some of these children home. So we, in our arrogance and our ignorance, decided to work with the parents of some of these children until more appropriate settings could be found. What we learned was pretty miraculous! We found that 84% percent of those youth could be kept at home with their own families if we correctly provided services to those families, which means if those services were intensive enough, were provided for a long enough time, included a 24-hour crisis intervention component, and, most importantly, if we asked the families what they needed and were willing to provide those services).

Now, the fact that so many young people would do so well at home amazed us, because we had formerly been convinced that these children could not live with their families and needed out-of-home placements. This resulted in a major shift in how we saw our job. The concept of supporting the families of the children sent to our agency became the backbone of our services. We came to believe that if you can plug in the right amount of services, even a family everyone had given up on can provide a better placement for a child than any other place in the best service system.

It was in the early to mid-1970s when we started offering these family-based services; and believe me, it was a real learning process for us. I can't tell you how overjoyed I was to go out to people's homes and to work with the families there. Being new at it, and it being a new process, I made a lot of mistakes.

At first, we created a traditional clinical model similar to the ones we had learned about in our training, in which we would tell parents what to do, and they were expected to do it. But they often *wouldn't* do it, and then we would blame them and say they were resistant to treatment.

This was Kaleidoscope, however. When things weren't working, we sat down and questioned our reaction to these parents. After a while, the reason it wasn't working, we concluded, was that we were trying to make decisions for them when what they really needed was the chance to make decisions for themselves. The lesson we have learned over the years is that families will most often make good decisions for themselves if we are able to give them the information, time, and processes for doing so. Many years later, we have come even further in our thinking and believe that services need to go beyond just "including" families; rather, we believe families themselves have to be the ones making decisions about the services that they and their children need.

Human services is the only avenue I'm aware of in which families do not have control of their lives. Were I to get a toothache, I would make the decision to go to a dentist, and he might tell me, "Karl, you need a root canal." If I didn't want a root canal, I would have choices: I could do nothing or I could go to another dentist. If I went to the doctor and he said, "Karl, you know, you really need some surgery," I would have the option of saying, "No, I don't think so," and choose to live without this surgery or go to another doctor to find another possible solution. But in human services, families don't have control. If families do not do what is recommended to them by the human services people, their children can be taken away from them. When families are allowed and encouraged to take control of their lives, I believe they can make positive changes. This strengths-based view of families became the backbone for our services.

At this early time in the history of Kaleidoscope, we were working with children, youth, and families in three environments: group homes, independent living services, and in-home services. Then I had a very strange experience, which led me to question the value of our group home services. At that time

I was running the agency alone. I did all of the agency planning and staff training, and my head had started to swell and I began saying to myself, "Wow, you're really on to something. You've really got this locked up."

At the same time, I was feeling besieged and struggling with a lot of people, including those from the state and other service providers. One day, I looked up and saw my whole staff coming down the hall. My fantasy was, "Oh boy, support at last, support at last! I bet these people are coming to give me an award."

I thought this through: "You know, I'm going to accept this award, but I really have to have the right amount of humility when I do it."

Unfortunately, they weren't coming to give me an award; they were coming to tell me they were tired of listening to me and that I needed to find someone else to do the trainings—someone who knew what the devil they were talking about. Now, I saw that I had one of two options as a response. I could fire all the staff who were there, or I could listen to them. Because I truly believe administrators have to listen to their staff, I saw this as an opportunity, and I chose to do what they had asked me.

I found a guy to do the trainings, and he was wonderful. But he came in, and the first word out of his mouth was "burnout." We all looked around and saw a room full of blank stares. Because we were working 60-plus hours a week and had been unable to keep up with the literature, none of us had ever heard of "burnout." He spent the next two hours explaining to us what burnout was and, as a result, we all burned out in those two hours! People slid down in their chairs, broke out in sweats, started to tremble. I myself rapidly came to the realization that, if you do not know what burnout is, it will not happen to you, but as soon as you learn about it, it will.

One guy, who ran one of the group homes, immediately walked up to me and said, "Karl, I can't take it anymore, I'm burned out."

"Well, I know how you feel," I said.

He continued, "You don't understand. I've got to get away from here for at least 30 days."

I said, "Uh-oh!" Because this meant that I would have to run his group home while he was gone.

Well, he was an incredible staff member. He had this ability to develop instant relationships with children. When you have a "No Reject-No Eject" policy, and you cannot make any decisions about who comes into your services and you cannot throw anyone out, the only way you get to move people from point A to point B is through your ability to develop relationships with them. So I wanted to keep him, and I told him he could have his 30 days off.

We had some really great people working at Kaleidoscope, but I had the same challenges that any other administrator has, and out of 75 staff, some of them were not so great. As a matter of fact, the same day, one of them walked up to me and said, "Hey, I heard you gave Roger 30 days off, and you need to know, I'm burned out."

My response to this person was, "Look, in order to burn out, first you've got to be on fire—and I've never seen you on fire!"

To get back to the point of this story, I happened to be at the group home the day Roger came back from his time off. We were sitting around after dinner and all the residents saw him at once. They loved him very much, so they all rushed out to greet him. The first two who reached him wrapped themselves around each of his legs. The next two grabbed his arms, and he looked just like a scarecrow. When the fifth one got to him and there were no arms or legs left to grab, he didn't know how to react. So, he got really excited and hauled off and hit Roger in the stomach! At that moment a light went off in my head. I thought, "You know Karl, maybe five youth in one place are too many!"

Inside of three months, we had closed all of the group homes and moved those young people into treatment foster care where we would place one in a home and have one parent relinquish employment. This taught us that when we individualize services in the home environment to the right degree, we can duplicate any of the most intensive services we have ever seen in group homes and residential treatment centers. Occasionally, a caseworker will come up to me and say, "Karl, this young man can't stand the intimacy of a foster home; he needs a group home."

I respond by saying, "Fine, I'll go out and find a family with four or five children and adolescents of their own, place your young man there, and surround him with staff. There! You have your group home! And it will be a group home that will offer him better peer relationships than most."

In the last group home I closed, three out of the five youth there had set fires: much of my gray hair came from that experience. I have never really understood why we seem to think there is something magical about putting young people who have the same issues together in the same program. You know, first we put all the children who have set fires together, and then we worry about what they are learning from each other. Even worse, we put all the sex offenders together, and we *know* what *they* have learned from each other! Grouping children and adolescents with the same issues is not normal, nor is it part of a normalization process. So we started to use treatment foster care. We ultimately found that we only needed three environments in which to provide services to all of the children and families referred to us if we could add in any additional individualized services a child needed. First, we would try to intervene in the home environment with in-home services, and if it didn't work, we had the option of offering services in our treatment foster care or independent living environments.

The individuation of our care in those three environments by folding in extra services when needed was one of the first of the Wraparound efforts in this country. Those interventions were extremely successful, not because we were so great at what we did, but because they were highly individualized. In the group homes, we found the more children we had in one place, the more time we spent on trying to stay in control and the less we were able to spend on treatment. I remember a particular occasion in one of our group homes when one of the boys "went off." As the staff started to restrain him, another boy "went off." We got really terrified that we were going to wind up with five boys in restraints on the floor. While my original thought as to the most appropriate way to deal with the first boy's outburst was to just walk away from him and let him settle down, I couldn't do this, because we couldn't afford to lose control. If there had only been one boy in the home, I could have risked losing control and would have just walked away. From then on, we only put boys and girls in environments in which we could individualize services, including just walking away, when it was the most appropriate thing to do.

After delivering individualized services in Chicago for about 15 years, an opportunity arose to apply the individualized service lessons we had learned at Kaleidoscope on a larger scale. I got a call from Dr. John VanDenBerg from Alaska; he said they were starting an initiative to better serve the state's children and adolescents. Alaska is the largest state in the union and also the richest. At that time, one did not pay taxes in Alaska; rather, the state paid you to live there. They had saved all the profits they made from oil and used the interest to run the state. Once when oil prices were down, they got terrified that they were going to have to spend some of the principal, and they looked around to see where they could save some dollars. One of the places they looked, of course, was in human services, where they saw they were sending many of their children to out-of-state facilities. John invited me to go with him to talk to the heads of the Alaskan state agencies that supported these placements.

We suggested to them that they could provide better services for children and adolescents, and save money at the same time. Now, one of the things I've learned about talking to bureaucrats is that they like to hear the magical phrase, "This is not going to cost you anything," which is basically what we said about Alaska. We said, "Look, if you would bring your youth back from those out-of-state facilities, the dollars will follow them back into Alaska. If you use Wraparound services, you will be able use to the money you saved to serve those children and have enough left over to serve the rest of the children in your system. In addition, you won't have to send them to institutions and residential programs." They decided they would try it.

We drew up individualized plans for all of those children and brought them back to the State of Alaska—all of them with exception of one came back in the first year. In five years, the use of Wraparound had literally saved Alaska ten million dollars and led to major changes in their service system. After that, a lot of states got really interested in this and started to provide Wraparound services. Dr. Barbara Burns of Duke University, a national expert on the evaluation of Wraparound programs, has estimated that there are now over 100,000 young people in some kind of Wraparound initiative in this country (1999).

My ethnic background is a mixture of African, Irish, Cherokee, and Black Feet. From all of those traditions my destiny has been to be storyteller—I get it from every part of my heritage. In this book, my stories about the individuals we had the pleasure to serve at Kaleidoscope and around the country will act as the foundation on which Ira and I will try to help you understand this Wraparound thing as it grew at Kaleidoscope. I will end this chapter by telling you a special story that captures the spirit of Wraparound.

Kaleidoscope had a call one day asking us to pick up a child who was HIV-positive. His dad was HIV-positive and so was his mom, and the child had been found with his parents in an abandoned building. After we picked up the baby, we immediately started to try to provide services to Dad and Mom. At first, they were not really interested in services, and it was really hard trying to get to know them. Eventually, however, their stories started to come out. Tyrone's story began when he went to Vietnam, where he spent his 18th birthday. While he was there, he learned how to take drugs! He liked them, and he continued to take them. He was discharged on the last day of 1968. This date was significant because the next day they started drug testing all of the vets coming back from Vietnam, so Tyrone avoided having his drug use detected and getting treatment for it.

He came home and started looking for a job. Well, he looked in the newspapers and the first thing that caught his eye was an ad from a pharmaceutical company looking for a sales representative. And he said, "Wow, that's right down my alley." He applied for the job, saying, "What the hell, I don't have anything to lose."

He fooled the machine and passed the lie detector test, and he started selling legitimate drugs. He told us, "You know, the ball really started rolling then. I thought I had taken drugs before, but then I had all of these drugs at my disposal, and I started taking all of them." He continued, "Karl, I started taking all of these drugs, and started stealing so much, that I got scared and quit the drug company before they caught me. But by then I had a habit, so I started stealing from trains in order to get enough money to pay for my habit. So, of course, I went to jail."

He talked about how he would go in and out of jail. So, I asked him, "Your girlfriend here, how long have you guys been together?"

He said "Fourteen years."

I said, "Fourteen years! You guys have been on drugs together for 14 years?"

He said, "Yeah. I've been going in and out of jail, she would wait for me and she was always there when I came back."

I started to think about the divorce rates in this country, and I started to think about how many people I know who would be willing to hang with someone for 14 years, sharing drugs and living in abandoned buildings: not a lot of people! I viewed Tyrone and Carol's relationship and the fact that they were there for each other as a strength.

We wound up getting them an apartment, substance abuse services, and some other stuff, and all of a sudden things started to look a little bit better. During this time, we learned that Tyrone was also really good at art, and he volunteered to do all of the artwork in our nursery. While he was doing that, he would come in and work with the little children, including his own child on the occasions when he visited. We discovered he was one of the best people we'd ever seen working with little children!

In 1993, Kaleidoscope hosted the Second International Wraparound Conference in Chicago. At its start, we held a large plenary session introducing Wraparound by highlighting several successful Wraparound efforts around the country. The several major speakers in this session were each preceded preceded by a video clip from one of the featured programs. Then, one of the family members from that video clip introduced the next speaker. When it was Kaleidoscope's turn, I asked Tyrone and Carol to participate. We put their story on video, after which they introduced the keynote speaker.

But while we were there, Tyrone came up and said, "Karl, I'm disappointed in you."

I asked him, "Why?"

And he replied, "Because you put a conference together for a thousand people and you don't have any place for people to hold AA Meetings."

I said, "Well, you're right."

He continued, "But I'll run some meetings if you want me to."

This was the start of Tyrone's career running AA meetings. He wound up as one of the most respected drug counselors and street counselors on the north side of Chicago. We respected his work, his intellect, and his efforts so much that we put him on Kaleidoscope's Board of Directors. We were so proud of him!

However well Tyrone did, we could never get Carol to say much of anything to us. She would say "hello" and such, but not much else. Then, Carol got sick and was hospitalized; sad to say, she was dying of AIDS. My wife and I went by to see her, and when we walked in the room the first thing we noticed was that Tyrone wasn't there. I got a little irritated. I said, "Carol, where the heck is Tyrone?"

She gave the usual type of Carol response: "He's not here."

I said, "Carol, I can see he's not here, but he should be. Where is he?"

Carol explained, "Well, Karl, this is the week that you guys sent all of the foster parents and biological parents to camp with the kids, and I thought it would be more important for Tyrone to be with our son at camp than it was for him to be here."

I said, "Wow." This was a woman who had many negative things written about her in the files, including having already had one child taken from her (we had looked for this child in the system and had not been able to find him), and whose other child was in foster care. I just looked at her! Here lying in the hospital dying was a person whom everyone believed didn't care about her children, and she felt it was more important for the one real support in her life to be with her child than there with her.

My wife, Kathy, and I just sat there fighting back tears. I turned to Carol and said, "Look, Carol, is there anything I can do for you?"

She thought about this for a while and said, "Yeah, you can make Tyrone marry me."

Kathy gave me a look, because she knows me and knew what was coming, and I did not disappoint her. I turned to Carol and said, "Do you mean to tell me that you would use death to trap this guy into marriage?"

Carol smiled. "Karl, I'd use anything that I could."

On our way home from the hospital, we went to City Hall and started the process to get a license. We had a little talk with Tyrone about what he needed to do and he was cool with it. They said it would take us three days to get a marriage license. One of our foster parents, who was a minister, agreed to come and perform the ceremony. When the three days had passed and we were finally going to get the marriage license, we got everybody into their fancy clothes and started putting things together. We scheduled the wedding for 3:00. Unfortunately, Carol died about 1:30. But we continued with the wedding because this had been Carol's last wish and we thought it was important to fulfill it for her. Tyrone is probably the only person in this country ever to get married to a dead person.

The story of Tyrone and Carol is special to me: it brings to life the power Wraparound can exert in peoples lives, including my own. Later in the book, Ira and I will point out some special lessons we think can be learned from this story, but for now, just let yourself get the feel of it. Each of the stories I tell in this book is equally special to me, for each of the individuals involved and their families have become integral parts of my life and experience. Ira and I hope they will be as special to you.

cindy

A Story About the Essence of Wraparound

In 1987, the State of Illinois approached Kaleidoscope, expressing a need for services for infants who were born HIV-positive or diagnosed with AIDS. Due to our prior experience, we accepted the challenge to create a more normalized environment, a home life, and a family for these abandoned children.

Kaleidoscope was informed by the state that most of the parents of the children with pediatric AIDS were drug abusers and prostitutes and were not interested in their children. Regardless, we believed strongly in the ties of families, and we knew we needed to look for these children's parents. In addition, we felt the family is more than just a mother and a father, and also consists of aunts, uncles, grandparents, and even close friends. Some cultures feel that the family includes the whole tribe or neighborhood. We saw these children's natural parents and families as valuable resources, and we went out to look for them. Finding the families of abandoned children is not an easy task, however. Those who have worked in in-home service programs know that every community has what we call "natural informants," or nosy people. These are the people who know everything going on in the neighborhood, and at Kaleidoscope, we tended to identify them when we tried to find someone in the community.

This particular time, we were looking for a woman named Cindy. The natural informant in this case was a man who ran a pawnshop. We left little notes for her there. These notes didn't clearly explain what we wanted because of our concern for Cindy's confidentiality and our expectation that the nosy informant would most likely open Cindy's mail. We left notes for three or four weeks. Eventually, Cindy called and asked what we wanted. We replied, "We want to know if you would like to see your baby." Cindy replied that she would, and we sent someone to pick her up.

Now, our office was a pretty relaxed place, clients and staff were always bringing in their children and pets. My office was at the end of a long hall, and on this particular day I smelled this horrendous odor. I went to see what it was—I thought someone had brought in a dog that had not had a bath in several years. As I got to the hall, the first thing I saw was a woman coming toward me. She was ragged. She was dirty. She had no teeth. I could tell she had no teeth because she had this great big smile on her face. As Cindy walked closer to me, I discovered it was she that I had been smelling.

I turned to her and said, "Hello." I have to confess, I was standing as far away from her as I possibly could and was holding my breath. She turned to me and mumbled something. In order to hear what she had said, it was necessary for me to move closer to her, which was a major challenge to my philosophy of unconditional care. When Cindy spoke again, I realized she was offering to perform certain sexual favors for me in exchange for money. Now, I believe that one of the quickest ways to break the ice with someone is through humor. So with a smile I said, "Cindy, this is something that we can't even talk about until you've had a bath and gotten some teeth in your mouth." I didn't know how she would react, but she began to laugh and I laughed with her. This was the beginning of a friendship (not an intimate relationship, I assure you), and a learning experience for both of us.

As I talked with Cindy, I decided that, as usual, a direct approach was best. I told her the information we had received suggested that she was a prostitute and a cocaine addict. I asked her how this had come about. She said she came from a small town down south and had lived on a farm for many years. She hated farming and had spent a lot of time in an effort to get away from it. She decided to head north, and after saving some money, got on a bus and headed for Chicago.

Things began to go wrong soon after she got off the bus. Cindy told me that in her hometown, people were very friendly; they shook hands and talked to each other on the street. When she tried this in Chicago, people shied away from her. They thought she was weird and looked at her strangely. Most people tend to do this in big cities, since not doing so could get a person seriously hurt or killed. Cindy's stomach began to hurt, and she got extremely anxious, so much so that it became difficult for her to talk. She lost her confidence, and as a result it took her a whole day just to find a room to live in.

The next morning she went out and attempted to find work. But every time she approached someone she again became anxious and nervous and couldn't talk. When she eventually became hungry and frustrated, she did not know where to seek help. I asked her if she had tried public aid, and she emphatically replied, "No!" Her family value was not to accept charity. So she continued to seek employment. Her job search being unsuccessful, she got to the point when she did have to swallow her pride and seek aid after all. In Cindy's hometown, she told me, there were only three people at the desks in the public aid office. They were friendly folks who would say "come on in" and "what can I do for you?" In Chicago, when she got to the public aid office early in the morning, she found a line stretching halfway around the block. It took hours for her to get in. By the time she was called, she was so nervous and anxious that once again she couldn't talk, and she ran out of the office.

Then, Cindy ran out of money. Hungry and on the verge of being homeless, she sold the last thing she had of value—her body. Because she hated doing this so much, the only way she could continue was to take drugs.

We at Kaleidoscope began to work with Cindy. We got her a bath, found her an apartment, and helped her get on public aid. We tried to get Cindy into a counseling program around AIDS, but she was in denial and had told us she didn't have AIDS.

After she was all set up and cleaned up, she told us she wanted to go into a drug abuse program. This irritated us, because *our* plan had called for us to develop a relationship with her first, before we approached her drug issues. Nothing seems to irritate service providers as much as when consumers get ahead of them. We're not in the habit of people telling us what to do; we're used to telling them. At Kaleidoscope, however, we believed in supporting people's desires to get better, and we arranged for her to enter a drug abuse program. Those of us who were optimistic bet she would complete it; those who weren't bet she wouldn't. We told Cindy that most people don't kick drugs with their first attempt, and that the problem with a lot of substance abuse programs is they will terminate you from the program if you reoffend while receiving services. Now we don't believe in doing business this way, because this is just the point in time when people need services the most. We told Cindy we hoped she would complete the service. But, in the event she wasn't successful, we assured her that we would still be here for her because our commitment to her was unconditional.

Cindy did successfully complete the program. When she returned to Kaleidoscope, she told us, the whole time she was away working on her drug issues, she thought about how Kaleidoscope had been so helpful to her, and she wondered if there was anything she could do for us. As she struggled to find a way to repay us, she remembered that the only thing we had asked her to do that she had refused was to seek counseling for AIDS issues. And, even though she "knew" she didn't have AIDS, she said she would go because we asked her to. She taught us that if we did the things people see as a priority, then they may be more willing to do some of the difficult things which we request of them.

A short time later, Cindy came to us and asked us how she was doing. We told her how proud we were of how far she had come. Her response shocked us. She said, "In that case, I want my baby back." Now, giving Cindy her baby back was not easy. Our first response was to remember that Cindy had been a prostitute and drug abuser and, perhaps she didn't deserve to have her baby back. We seemed to immediately forget about our philosophy, which states that if you can plug in enough services to support a family, even parents that most people would consider inadequate can care for their children better than the best substitute system can. Our faith in our beliefs and in Cindy prevailed, however, and we agreed to petition the state for the return of her child.

Not long afterward, Cindy once again challenged our beliefs when she told us she had come to understand she had no resources or family other than Kaleidoscope in Chicago, and that, to progress further, she would need the help of her family. As a result, she wanted to take her child and move back to her home in the South where she understood the people and their customs. As you may imagine, this was also a difficult adjustment for some of the staff. Not only was Cindy requesting her child back, she was now expressing her intention to remove the baby from our sphere of influence, beyond our ability to support her. This made it really rough for some of the staff to help Cindy make plans for moving out-of-state, but we knew it was the right thing for both her and us.

Beyond our fears of loss of control over her, making plans for Cindy's move was difficult for a number of reasons. The first was that she was white and the baby was biracial. The second was that she wanted to live back on the farm with her sister and brother-in-law, but they had personal safety concerns about her AIDS, a response that, unfortunately, is not at all unusual. As we worked to overcome these issues involved in moving, we got in touch with some agencies from Cindy's home state and asked them to help us. We brought the sister and brother-in-law to Chicago and worked with them in great depth. Although they continued to have some reservations, we reached a compromise in which her sister and brother-in-law would continue to live in the house, and Kaleidoscope would attempt to find the funds to help Cindy purchase a trailer so that she and her baby could also live on the farm. The state agreed to offer the necessary services to all members of the family. Under these arrangements, we felt comfortable that, eventually, this family would be able to function as a unit.

One of the planned supports was for Cindy to receive SSI benefits. As you may know, the process for this most often requires a great deal of time and a number of appeals. So by the time her benefit was approved, she was given notice that she had a lump sum of $6,000 in back payments coming to her. Once again, Cindy created a philosophical dilemma for the staff. Some felt she would take the money and buy cocaine; others felt she would take the money and do something productive. According to our beliefs, we worked through our feelings about Cindy being given such a large amount of money. We sat down with her and told her we hoped she would do something productive with this money. We also added, "In the event that you spend all of the money on cocaine, and if you are still alive, we will still be here for you. Our commitment to you is unconditional." Cindy never said a word; she left, and went to cash the check. She kept a small amount for herself and bought her trailer with the rest. Remember, Cindy's family value was not to accept charity. The plan was working. We were supporting Cindy's strengths and she rewarded our faith by not stumbling on her weaknesses.

Two weeks before Cindy was to move, she became sick from AIDS, went into the hospital, and died. I lost a friend, but more than that I also lost a teacher. The most important thing that Cindy taught me was that regardless of what you read, hear, or think about people, you shouldn't give up on them. There are a lot of Cindys in this world, and if we can learn to listen to them with open hearts and open minds, then the children and families will get better.

Lessons from Cindy About What Wraparound Is

Cindy's story describes the essence of Wraparound and the individualized service approaches as developed by Karl Dennis and Kaleidoscope. To Karl, Cindy was not a patient, not a reclamation project, not the object of a missionary endeavor. No, to Karl, Cindy was a friend. A basic aspect of Karl's approach is that to help other people, one has to forge a bond with them that goes beyond that of a traditional therapeutic contract. To trust a person offering help, families and individuals in need must develop a relationship with that person that is built on mutual respect and caring.

Many mental health and other human service professionals may not agree with this premise. In more traditional therapeutic theories, the therapist is encouraged to hide his or her personality as much as possible, and a real relationship between the therapist and the "patient" is thought to interfere with progress in therapy.[1] Therefore, professionals who are learning about the principles and practice of Wraparound services often have a strong negative reaction to the suggestion that they need to be Cindy's friend if they are going to help her; they might even worry that being her friend will get in the way. Long-term experience at Kaleidoscope, however, has taught us that liking people and being perceived as a friend facilitates interventions with both youth and families. A research study by Dr. John Whitbeck (personal communication, 1991) on home-based services in the State of Washington found that when professionals were asked why their service worked, they most always pointed to some moment in which a family or a family member had some great insight into the problems and the solutions. When the families who were receiving help were asked how the service helped them, however, most pointed to a more personal interaction that reflected caring, such as, "I remember the day when he helped me move!"

Are the two approaches, friend or professional, incompatible? Probably not. It is relatively accepted practice for professionals to share some facts about their private lives with children and adolescents to gain their trust and facilitate the development of a therapeutic relationship with them. Children and adolescents can tell if their therapist likes them. They often refer to therapists as "their friends," and within these relationships, even formal psychotherapies can flourish. Although this is not usually the practice with adults and families, our experience with people like Cindy and with family preservation and other supportive interventions tells us that it works. The more complex an individual's troubles, the more likely that a friendly, supportive approach will be useful in working with him or her.

Being a friend doesn't mean bringing everyone home for dinner. It doesn't mean developing romantic or intimate relationships. It means letting people know that you care about them, that you respect them as

---

[1] Within Wraparound services, the word "patient" is not often used because of its medical connotation that the person has a disease that needs to eradicated. Instead, the individualized service approach sees itself as offering care to a person, an individual, or—in the more formal sense—a consumer. In this book, the word "patient" will always appear in quotes to signify the differences between the medical and more person-oriented service models.

human beings, and that you recognize their struggles to make things in their lives and the lives of their families work out better. If you don't like young people or their parents, you probably shouldn't work with them, because it will be hard for you to support them to the degree necessary. On the other hand, it should also be noted that in certain psychotherapies, more formal boundaries are useful, if not essential, to allow the therapy to proceed. When the individual or family has more complex needs that include some traditional psychotherapy, one should view the formal psychotherapy as one part of a larger service package in which the necessary supportive services are primary.

The second lesson that emerges from Cindy's story is that Karl saw her as his teacher. This occurred on two levels. On one level, Karl let Cindy teach him about herself. On the other level, he also learned lessons from her on how to best help all people. Neither of these types of lessons fits well in a professional world that operates on the premise that our job is to use *our* knowledge to change other people's behavior. Wraparound and individualized service delivery require the opposite perspective—one that reflects the premise that no one knows a person better than him or herself, and that no one knows a child as well as his or her parent. The job of the professional is to learn from individuals and family members about those things that are important in their lives and to build personalized helping interventions in which the clients help themselves. To be truly effective, we must then apply our professional theory and clinical understanding of individuals and families in a way that reflects the individual's or family's understanding of itself.

What lessons did Cindy teach Karl about herself? He learned that the package someone comes in doesn't always reflect what is inside. Once Cindy felt accepted, was fed and got cleaned up, she demonstrated many hidden aspects of herself. Instead of a smelly and impudent drug-addicted prostitute, she taught us that she was really a simple, frustrated, and lost country girl who was over her head in the big city. She was undone not by some wicked streak, but merely as a result of her shyness and naiveté. She taught Karl about her sense of humor, about her strong values, and about the strength and determination that she couldn't use until after she had the support necessary to survive her environment.

Cindy's lessons also taught Karl a great deal about how to serve people in need. She taught him the basic elements of Wraparound services. The first of these reflected that taking a *strength-based* approach toward Cindy was a better strategy than focusing on her weaknesses. Time and time again, Karl and his staff faced decisions in which they either had to rely on Cindy to do the right thing or they had to protect her (and themselves) from her potential to mess things up. Each time, the staff was divided. When Cindy wanted to go into a drug program "too soon," they let her prove that she could do it, rather than focusing on the possibility that she would fail. They planned with her to get her baby back when that was her desire, and they allowed her to spend her SSI funds any way she chose. They learned to accept that when Cindy made requests, she did so out of her strengths and, if they supported those strengths, things would work out positively.

Most programs in our service system do not take that perspective, and most professional schools do not teach it. Rather, they focus on making assessments of weaknesses and the development of intervention plans aimed at ameliorating specific diagnoses. As a result, most attempts at helping people are aimed at their weaknesses and never allow them to demonstrate their strengths. We often refuse to look at anything but the problems people have, and then we blame them for not doing better. This flies in the face of a more logical understanding that when people have long-term, serious problems, we can only help them by supporting them to overcome their weaknesses with strengths.

One of the ways to ensure the provision of strength-based services is to have an *outcome-driven* intervention approach. What this means is that when Cindy asked the Kaleidoscope staff how she was doing, they had determined in advance what a positive outcome of their intervention with Cindy would be. (The best practice would have been for Cindy to have helped determine what this measure of outcome would be.) In this case, they told her she was doing well, which was based on a prior determination of what "well" would mean. The initial goals were very modest—for a relationship to have developed between Cindy and the staff. Given their first experience with her, this may have seemed like a very ambitious objective. Setting such a realistic goal afforded Cindy the luxury of not having to be "cured" before being successful. In addition, it allowed the staff to have a reasonable objective on which to judge both Cindy's progress and their performance. Just as important, it offered Kaleidoscope, as an agency, a way in which to justify their intervention to their funding source.

His experience with Cindy reaffirmed Karl's belief in *unconditional care*. When the staff trusted that Cindy's strength would allow her to successfully complete a drug abuse program, plan for her baby's return, or spend her money wisely, they did so within the context that, if she failed, they would be there to help her make the next step. What would have happened if she had failed and the care was not unconditional? Traditionally, she would have been considered a failure, or worse, a resistant failure. In the delivery of human services, we frequently blame people—or more specifically, people's weaknesses—for failing. And very often, that failure is used as an excuse to declare the individual "untreatable" and give up on them.

With unconditional care, we never give up! This premise comes with the understanding that, to grow, people have to try new and difficult things. And further, when trying new things, people often stumble. Only when care is unconditional will people feel comfortable enough to try something in which they might fail, because they have the knowledge that we will be there to catch them, help them up, and support them in trying again. It's like helping a baby learn to walk. If we were to give the baby away each time it fell, the risk of failure would soon overcome the child's desire to walk. Luckily, parents understand the need for an unconditional approach to this type of falling down. Cindy teaches us that we need to approach people in a similarly unconditional way when they stumble over more grown-up tasks.

Cindy also teaches that we need to be *culturally competent.* She came from a background that was alien, not only to Chicago, but to the staff of Kaleidoscope. Before Karl could help Cindy give up her troubled life, he had to understand how she got where she was. That required that he learn what it is like to be a poor White girl from the rural South, what it meant for someone from that background to go to a big city, and what it meant to have had Cindy's personally significant Chicago experiences. Most service providers deliver services within the framework of their own personal background, as modified by the helping approach taught in their training programs. Many of us were never trained about the importance of understanding the role of a person's culture in the expression of his or her problems and in how to best support him or her. Yet, an individual's cultural and ethnic backgrounds are vital factors in how they react to their world and in how they will respond to different interventions. Cindy understood that she would be better off living in the community where she developed her style and values, and where those strengths would be assets to her.

Cindy needed a *community-based* intervention. She told Karl that she had no friends or relatives in Chicago, where Kaleidoscope was her only visible support. While Karl and the staff were worried that they couldn't support her if she moved back down south, Cindy let them know that, unconditional as it was, Kaleidoscope was only an agency. True independence would require that she live in a place where her family, friends, and other people whose ways she understood were available to her. Traditionally, we have taken youth out of their families and out of their communities on the basis that families were part of a child's problem and that a more formally structured environment was curative. We place children in "good" places, which may not prepare them to return to useful lives in their communities. Cindy lets us know that she had more natural supports in her own world than we could ever create for her in ours.

Cindy also felt she could survive better living with her family. And so, she taught us that care must be *family-focused*—that we must reserve a major role for family members to determine their own needs, and that we must focus on the whole family rather than on just one individual. We must learn to understand that supporting family members in helping each other makes the most sense. Once she felt supported, Cindy was able to tell us what she and her baby needed. She understood that it was not only important for her to care for her own child, but it was equally important for her to be able to take advantage of the support available in her own family. This was true even though her sister and her husband were afraid of Cindy's AIDS, not entirely accepting of her biracial baby, and needed help to understand their role in supporting Cindy and overcoming those feelings that were getting in the way of their full support. To help Cindy, we needed to help her whole family. Cindy helped teach us that she would be able to flourish more easily with her family in a community where she felt comfortable and in which she understood their ways. In her life she had struggled with both her family and her community. Her lifestyle had led her baby to struggle also. Yet, she understood that Kaleidoscope would always be an institution of a sort, and both she and her baby would be supported best in the context of Cindy's family and community.

In working with Cindy, Karl learned that one agency could not be of help to her alone, that an *interagency approach* was necessary. At a minimum, Cindy needed substance abuse support for her addictions, medical support for her and her child's AIDS, public assistance and SSI for her financial needs, and she and her family needed counseling to help with her transition home. Each of these forms of help came from different community agencies. None of this care was provided in a way that was coordinated, rather it was most likely provided out of context with the others. In addition, as we heard in the story, Cindy was not very good at navigating even one of these agencies without help. Imagine how difficult it would have been for her to work with all of them—all at the same time. Someone, in this case Kaleidoscope, had to help her access them, and make sure that all of the help fit and worked together for Cindy's benefit. It would have been even better if all of those agencies had come together before Cindy came along and found a way to work jointly so that people with cross-agency needs could easily get all those needs met.

Of course, it was not Kaleidoscope as an agency that brought it all together; rather the agency convened a group of people who could work together to help Cindy—a *Child and Family Team.* Cindy taught Kaleidoscope over and over again that she knew what was best for herself and her baby. Although the staff often questioned her judgment, when they supported her in doing what she thought was right, it worked. Cindy could not, however, make it work all by herself. She needed the support of Kaleidoscope staff and others in her life and community to make it happen. The Child and Family Team is the practical mechanism for supporting the strengths and meeting the needs of an individual and/or family in Wraparound. In Cindy's case, the team was small. At first, it included only Kaleidoscope staff. Later it came to include her baby's worker and her family. Each individual's Child and Family Team is unique to his or her needs, and it comprises all those individuals who are working with that person, with a focus on those who care about him or her and those who have resources to offer. It is the team's job to help the client elucidate his or her needs and develop a plan for meeting those needs. The team also plays a role in finding the resources to support the plan and in making it happen.

A lesson that the whole service community gained from Cindy's experience was that the best care was also *cost effective.* They learned that the Kaleidoscope approach to Cindy and her baby had the potential to reduce costs markedly. If Cindy had lived, one major cost savings would have been to avoid long-term hospitalization, or other forms of institutionalization, for her baby. Further saving would have come from the normalization of Cindy's life and her ability to become more self-sufficient and less of a burden on society. In addition, although we are not good at figuring the cost of social problems, it can be assumed that, by getting an addicted, HIV-infected prostitute off drugs and off the streets, a major cost savings would occur for each individual whom she did not infect with AIDS.

Once Karl had been taught all of these lessons, Cindy helped him put it all together. He learned that to best help people, he had to take an *individualized approach*. Having learned who she was inside, Karl and Kaleidoscope worked with Cindy to develop a unique approach based on her strengths and cultural background and which was aimed at supporting her both *as* a family and *in* a family within her natural community. And most important of all, Karl and his staff committed themselves unconditionally to providing the help and support Cindy needed. In the end, Karl and Cindy both found friends.

The chapters of this book that follow will detail the basic elements of the Wraparound service approach:

- A practice of unconditional care;

- A focus on individual strengths;

- A family-driven, family-strengths-focused process;

- An individualized approach;

- An emphasis on serving families within their communities;

- A commitment to culturally competent care;

- A process that uses Child and Family Teams;

- An emphasis on interagency collaboration;

- A net result of cost effectiveness; and

- An outcome-driven process.

These elements are presented in an order that seemed to flow best as this book was written, and do not reflect a hierarchy of importance.

alex and shirley

A Story About Family Focus and Family Strengths

One of the families I was fortunate enough to work with was Alex's. He had gotten into trouble at school because he beat up other children. So when he was 13, the school system put Alex in a residential placement—where he continued to beat up other children. Over time, he was moved from one placement to another—and in each, he continued to beat up other children. When he reached the age of 15 and put on some weight, Alex stopped beating up children and started to beat up staff members of the facilities where he had been placed. For this, he wound up in corrections.

As expected, while he was in the juvenile justice placement he got in a fight with another young man. The two were separated, and Alex was thrown in a solitary confinement room that had doors made of solid oak held together with steel strips. Alex was very disappointed with this decision, and he decided he did not want to be there, so he physically tore the door off the hinges and came out.

Two weeks later, the people at the juvenile justice agency decided Alex had "maximized his stay in corrections" and he became one of three children I have worked with in my career who were actually kicked out of jail. Their position was that, evidently, Alex had a mental health problem; anyone who could tear a door from its hinges had to have a mental health problem. So, they sent him to Mental Health and a turf war began.

Mental Health said, "Oh no! Not us! He was originally placed through Education, so he's an Education child." So, Juvenile Justice then sent him back to Education. Education, having unsuccessfully provided services to Alex before, did not want to try again. So they sent him to Social Services. Social Services looked over their shoulder to see where they could send Alex, and there was no one left.

Being stuck, Social Services began to look for a placement for Alex. Considering his history, what he was capable of, and the fact they really didn't want to work with him, they started to look for placements in California, Texas, Florida, and Maine—as far away from Chicago as they possibly could. We tend to do this with those children who are aggressive and considered to be dangerous. When nobody else would take him, Kaleidoscope was asked if we would get involved with Alex, and having a "No Reject" policy, we did.

As I looked at his files, the one thing that stood out the most was that Shirley, his mother, had visited him twice a month, no matter where he was. At the time I got involved, it was taking her two and a half hours to get to the correctional facility—a trip that required her to take three buses. She did this twice a month, which suggested to me that she really cared about Alex.

Based on this one fact, when Alex's state social service caseworker asked what Kaleidoscope was going to do with Alex, I said we were going to send him home to his mother. The caseworker started to get angry, saying this was crazy and this young man was going to hurt someone. He called me a few names and said that we could not send Alex home. He then called Shirley and said, "Some fool named Karl Dennis is going to come by and try to talk you into taking Alex back home. Don't do it!""

She replied, "I'm not going to do it! I can't take care of Alex."

It was my job then to go and try to convince her that yes, maybe we could send Alex home. The first time I saw Shirley, she was standing on her porch. She had one hand holding the screen door and the other hand on her hip. The first words out of her mouth were, "Boy, he is not coming home!"

I said, "Yes, ma'am, but I just need a few minutes to talk to you."

Shirley replied, "Boy, I don't want to talk to you. He's not coming home!"

So, I used an intervention that has never failed me. I reached up and wiped my brow and said, "Do you think that I could have a glass of water? I'm awfully warm." No one has ever turned me down. The dangerous part of this intervention comes when the person goes in to get the water and I follow him or her into the house. Now, if you want to try this, let me give you some advice. If the person turns around and is frowning, run like hell. But, if they look confused, or unsure, hold your ground, because this means you have a chance. When I followed Shirley, she didn't chase me out.

So, the next thing I did, as always, was to look around for something to compliment her on. I never lie, and I never fail to find something I like. I said, "That's really a nice picture."

She was not impressed. "Drink your water and get out," she said.

"Yes ma'am," I responded, "but you need to know that it's my job to spend 10 or 15 minutes with you. I understand you can't do it today, so I'll be back tomorrow. If you can't do it tomorrow, then I'll come back the next day, and if you can't do it the next day, then I'll come back the day after that. I'll just keep coming back until we get to spend 10 or 15 minutes together. But if you do it today, you can get rid of me." Shirley reluctantly agreed to spend 10 or 15 minutes with me.

What I chose to tell her first was, "It's very clear to me that you care about Alex."

She said, "Yes, but he can't stay at home."

"Yes, ma'am," I replied, "and I know there is no way in the world that I can provide the services you need in order to keep Alex at home. But, if you tell me what those services would look like, maybe I could develop those services and we can serve another family. I believe you know exactly what you need to be able to keep Alex at home." So after we dickered back and forth for a little while, she finally agreed to tell me what services she needed.

I used to carry a Lucite stick with me that had glitter in it; I called it a magic wand. I liked to wave it and say, "Let's pretend things are magic and you could get anything, no matter what you asked for. Just tell me what you need and would ask for, if you had unlimited resources."

I waved the wand and Shirley said, "You know, when Alex was at home, we'd get up in the morning and Alex would say that he did not want to go to school. He knew if he procrastinated long enough, I would have to leave to go to work."

I said, "Yes, ma'am. Suppose we had a couple of guys who would come by each morning and their job would be to get Alex up and get him to school. How would that be?"

She replied it would be pretty good.

I waved the wand again and asked what else she needed. She answered, "When Alex would go to school, a lot of times he would get into trouble. The school would phone me and ask me to please get up there and see about my son. They suggested that if I didn't come right away, I didn't care about Alex. In the meantime, my boss would be standing behind me, and he would be saying that I had taken a lot of days off from work, and maybe I didn't care about my job."

I said, "Okay. All of the children we have served at Kaleidoscope are now back in schools in their own communities, whether they are in regular schools or alternative schools. We have learned to go to the schools and sit down with the principals, counselors, and teachers, and ask them, 'What do you need in order to keep this child in school? If it means putting a person with the child throughout the day, if it means only half a day of school and doing something else for the rest of the day, we are willing to provide that.' I think that if we talked to the school officials about Alex, we could develop the same kind of plan which would allow them to keep him in school." Shirley thought this made sense.

I waved the wand again and asked what else she needed. She said, "Well you know, Alex needs therapy, but unfortunately, he doesn't like it. Alex learned a long time ago that if you threaten to kill the therapist, and seem very sincere about it, the therapist will probably discharge you."

I told her I knew some therapists who would guarantee to work with Alex for at least a couple of years. To get that guarantee, I would agree to put someone in the room with Alex and the therapist—someone who is bigger than Alex and bigger than the therapist. It would be this person's job to keep Alex and the therapist from killing each other. As I mentioned in Chapter 1, we used to call those people "Friendly Gorillas," but now, when we put them in with a therapist, we call them "cotherapists" so we can bill Medicaid for their services.

So I waved the wand again and asked her what else she needed and she replied, "I have to tell you that Alex's problems are all my fault. I used to return home from work and I didn't have the patience that I normally have."

I asked Shirley to describe how this happened, and she told me how she would come home, start to cook dinner, and Alex would start to pick at her. "It would get me very upset," she related, "and to tell the truth, I felt that I was the one who set Alex off."

I said, "Suppose we pick Alex up from school every day. We know he needs tutoring and recreation. So maybe we can pick him up and do some tutoring for him and play some basketball and do some other sports with him. We won't bring him home until seven or eight o'clock in the evening and when we bring him home, we will have used the greatest intervention known to child care."

She asked, "What is that?"

I replied, "When he gets home, he will be as tired as hell. Tired children do not cause problems. I learned that from my grandmother."

Shirley laughed and I waved the wand again and she said, "You know, all this stuff sounds good, but the real problem we have here is that Alex is dangerous, and he is going to hurt someone, and it's probably going to be me!"

I said, "Well, yes, ma'am. You know, most parents can tell me when their children are getting ready to go off. Can you tell when Alex starts to escalate?"

She replied that she could tell almost two hours ahead of time.

I said, "Suppose that anytime you called, I could guarantee to have someone here within 45 minutes and who would stay as long as they were needed?"

"Yeah, right!" she challenged. "What about in the middle of the night?"

I replied, "Yes, ma'am, even in the middle of the night."

"Well what about weekends?" she continued. "You professionals don't like to work on weekends."

"Yes, ma'am, even on weekends."

She said, "What about holidays?"

"Yes ma'am, holidays, also."

So, I waved the wand again and asked her what else would she need. Shirley replied that she could not think of anything else. I said, "In that case, would Monday be too soon for Alex to come home?"

Alex did go home and we plugged in all the services for him that we had promised. It wasn't easy. We spent a lot of time at school and a lot of time at his home in the middle of the night. We did this for almost three years, but it was worth it. Alex was a child whom no institution or residential program in the country was willing to admit, and we were able to keep him at home with his own family.

It is important to understand that I didn't design Alex's intervention, his mother did. Shirley told me what it was she needed, and that's what we provided.

Lessons About Being Family Focused and Tapping Family Strengths

To me, Alex and Shirley's story has always been magic. It was the first story that I heard Karl tell and, to me, represents the essence of Wraparound. I got so hung up on the magic wand that Karl bought me one several years later. But my magic wand was merely a Lucite stick. The real magic in the story is Karl's faith in Shirley. That faith defines an underlying principle of individualized services, the need for a family focus based on each family's strengths.

First, picture Shirley. Remember her worry that, when she came home from work tired and cranky, she "set Alex off." She was not alone, for it is not unusual for mothers to blame themselves for their children's problems. Parents who have struggled with their youngster's troubling behaviors, often from birth, feel that they should be able to meet their child's needs. When they can't, they may feel that any problem an infant or young child has is the result of their inability to make things right. This is true even when children have physical problems. Many parents feel they have failed their sick children, in spite of professionals telling them that there was nothing they did wrong or could have done differently. When the problems are emotional and/or behavioral, often there is no one to help parents see that what has happened is not their fault.

The more parents blame themselves, the more others join in the blaming. Sometimes this happens within the family itself. Many times a father's response to a child with troubles is to blame the mother. "It's your job to bring up this child, why can't you do it right?" Similar responses can come from grandparents, aunts, and uncles, other relatives, and even old family friends. This can lead a mother to blame herself even more, causing further family tension.

In families with emotionally unique children, family tension is inevitable. As Shirley pointed out, when tensions grew in her family, things got worse. Her impression was that *her* crankiness "set Alex off." As with many troubled children, it is more likely that Alex's behavior led to tension in the household to which he reacted poorly, which is what really set him off. To complicate things further, his problematic behavior then led to more tension in the family. This circular kind of struggle can cause a family to react poorly. No wonder when outsiders look into families with troubled children, they see trouble. Traditionally, this type of family reaction has been labeled as "dysfunctional." The dysfunction, however, is a better descriptor of the response of professionals, relatives, and friends to a family's attempts at managing a child with a unique set of needs. Yes, the family often appears to be floundering, but, for many years their cries for help have either gone unheeded or been met with inadequate, often dead wrong, responses. No wonder Shirley blamed herself. It was a natural motherly response to a child with troubles. In addition, the helping community had done nothing to change her mind; worse, they encouraged her to accept that burden.

Next, picture Shirley through the eyes of the agencies that had placed her son in institutions. Professionals are not always great at helping parents ask for help. In fact, sometimes professionals unwittingly reinforce parents' self-blame. Many well-meaning pediatricians and well-baby clinics tell parents, especially mothers, who sense that something is wrong with an infant, "If you could only relax, your baby would be fine." In other words, "It's your fault that your baby is acting up." Over the years, as the children develop in unique ways, parents who fail to receive needed help are less and less able to find answers as to how to best meet their children's needs.

Rather than seeing a caring mother who was caught between the demands of her troubled son and an unsympathetic boss, and therefore was unable to meet Alex's complex needs, the agencies saw a burned-out woman who appeared to be unable to control her son. They bought into and reinforced Shirley's negative belief that she had brought on Alex's problems through her behavior. The agencies saw Alex as irreparably broken, with a mother too dysfunctional to ever care for him. Within that context, the only choice was to institutionalize Alex and keep him away from home.

The magic in Alex and Shirley's story was Karl's ability to see past the 15 years of blaming in Shirley's life, which resulted, in part, from her negative experiences with the public agencies entrusted with Alex's care. Regardless of the mess that he saw, Karl focused on one vital fact—the family's greatest strength was that Shirley cared! Karl looked past her unsuccessful responses to Alex's behavior, looked past the behaviors themselves, he even looked past her initial negative response to his visit. He focused on one thing: no matter where her son was, or how difficult it was to get there, she visited him regularly.

Alex was a youth who had very little going for him. He appeared to be unable to control his behaviors, and nobody could control them for him. He had defeated every program he had ever been in, including being kicked out of jail. One aspect of his life was glaringly positive, however: his mother's love. Yet this, his only resource, was not only being ignored, it was being undermined. The agencies had taught Shirley that she had nothing to offer her child and that he could only be helped by institutional care. They validated her fears that, at best, she couldn't help him, and, at worst, his problems were all her fault.

Karl did just the opposite. He encouraged Shirley to see herself as the most important resource that Alex had. Karl believed that her love for Alex was the pivotal factor in helping her child. With one short comment, "I see that you care for Alex," Karl gave her credit for all of her years of struggling for and with her son.

Karl proposed interventions based on her understanding and her needs. He let her know that he appreciated how hard it had been to live with Alex and to try to help him. He helped her believe that the reason she had failed to help her son was that no one had helped her meet his special and unique needs—needs that no parent could have been able to meet alone. He did this by giving her credit for knowing what Alex needed. He encouraged her to give her assessment of Alex's needs, and he listened to her answers.

Shirley and Karl built a treatment plan around her family and its strengths. This demonstrates why a family focus is one of the underlying principles of Wraparound services. Every family has strengths—your family, my family, even families that do not appear to be doing well. It is those strengths that keep us going. When we see those strengths as a resource, we can use them to help a family overcome its problems, especially the problems that follow from living with a child with unique emotional responses. If we ignore those strengths, we force ourselves to view the family from the point of view of its problems, as weak and helpless. We box them out of being intervention resources and put ourselves in the position of having to do all of the work necessary to help meet the needs of their children. We deny ourselves—and the children—what is probably the most important resource.

By focusing on the family's strengths, Karl provided Alex with the support of the person who cared for him the most. The key was to bolster the family with adequate supports. Karl asked, "What can I do to help you support Alex?" Shirley knew. In the space of 10 to 15 minutes, she and Karl developed an intervention plan far more powerful than those from any of the institutions in which Alex had been placed.

Alex and Shirley's story makes the further point that, in addition to the fact that Karl had faith in Shirley's strengths, he also believed that she knew better than anyone what Alex needed. Karl says, "I didn't design Alex's intervention, Shirley did." This powerful statement drives home the value that Karl gives to this parent's knowledge of her child. Shirley's impressions of her child were acknowledged as important. She had lived and struggled with him for many years and had an intimate understanding of what he needed. She may have needed Karl to help her articulate those needs and/or to design an effective intervention, but it was her concerns that were addressed. This made her feel better about herself and confirmed the part of her that believed that she had done the best she could do for Alex; it also diminished the part of her that felt that she had ruined him. An additional effect of having Shirley be the major architect of Alex's intervention is that it said she was strong and wise enough to be a valued partner in her son's care. This partnership was very important in that it assured her participation in making the plan happen. She learned to trust her observations and the role they played in helping the intervention team make decisions. Having been listened to and supported, Shirley was willing to trust the suggestions of others and let her son come home. She learned that Karl and the rest of his team really did think she was strong and vital to Alex's future. And she proved them correct.

Although Alex's family required a lot of services and supports for him to live at home, Karl did not see this need for such intensive service as a family weakness; he saw it as a reality. After all, Alex had so many troubles that no agency was willing to accept him into its program. In Alex's home, Karl developed a degree of service that institutions would have found necessary but were unwilling to provide. Karl and Kaleidoscope's success was their recognition that they could not do this difficult job alone and they must utilize Alex's family.

Sometimes the strength in a family does not include the capacity to have the child live at home. This occurs when the child's needs outstrip the family's capacity to cope and the community's ability to support the child at home. There are several types of situations in which this might be true. Many times the situation is temporary, as when a child's problems require an acute short-term hospitalization, or when a family is exhausted from dealing with a troubled child's unrelenting problems and a short respite period is needed. Some families may not be appropriate full-time caretakers for their children over a longer period of time, due to a multitude of factors. But even in these rare instances, the family strengths need to be realized and used to help meet the child's needs. (A good example is Karl's story of Tyrone and Carol, which he told in the first chapter of this book.)

Many professionals have trouble accepting a family-focused approach. This probably describes you if you feel that Karl was pandering to or catering to Shirley's desires. When I tell Alex's story, and I do, I ad lib by adding that, when told that she could call for help, Shirley said, "That would be good, but I can't afford a phone." To the truly family-focused professional, the addition of a telephone as part of the intervention package is very easy to accept. To the skeptic, a telephone goes beyond the boundaries of treatment and is usually seen as a handout, rife with the potential for misuse or even fraud. When we truly believe that families can be equal partners in caring for their unique children, we must listen to all of their requests with equal understanding. In one situation, to prevent the institutionalization of a child, the employer agreed, in partnership with other community resources, to build the family a new house better suited to the care of the child at home. To the truly family-focused professional, this approach makes a lot of sense.

Some very important things have happened over the last 25 years to aid professionals in accepting parents as equal partners and to help parents play a greater, more important role in helping their children. In 1984, the federal government began a nationwide program aimed at assisting states and communities to better meet the needs of families with children like Alex. It was called the Child and Adolescent Service System Program, CASSP, and one of its goals was to encourage state governments to increase the role of parents in caring for their children and in planning the system in which that care was delivered. Some of the states that got these federal grants (by 1996, all 50 states had received them), used these funds to support the development of parent support and advocacy groups. At the same time, the federal government worked with one of its technical-assistance resources in Portland, Oregon, named the Research and Training Center for Family Support and Children's Mental Health, to produce a number of regional conferences, called Families As Allies, which brought together parents and professionals involved with the care of children and adolescents with severe emotional disturbances.

The Families As Allies meetings were very exciting, and the power that grew from them ultimately led to the development of two national parent-driven organizations. One of these was the national Federation of Families for Children's Mental Health, or more commonly the Federation, which is an organization of both family members and professionals who are concerned with increasing the degree to which families can get involved in the care and planning for their children with unique needs. The other group was a child-focused outgrowth of the National Alliance for the Mentally Ill, or NAMI, called the Child and Adolescent Network, or NAMI-CAN. As a result, parents around the country have an increasing access to support and advocacy through both Federation- and NAMI-sponsored local groups.[1] How different things might have been for Shirley if she had had the support of other family members and professionals in her attempts to help her son in the years before Karl and Kaleidoscope came into her life?

Karl's family focus is not the only magic in Alex and Shirley's story. For Alex to be brought home, someone had to believe that his behavior was controllable. Karl did this by normalizing it. Karl was not surprised when Alex beat up children in an institution; after all, he had beaten up children at home. Karl realized that it was not a failure for Alex that he had not stopped his troubled behavior; rather, it was the failure of those programs, which had not helped Alex to grow. In the past, the system had blamed Alex. Instead, Karl gave credit to Alex for being Alex. As Alex got older and bigger and began to beat up adults, Karl again saw this as just Alex being Alex. To Karl, this pattern was not a sign of irreparable trouble; it was simply seen as Alex's way of doing things. In planning to bring Alex home to Shirley, Karl expected him to have trouble with hitting people, and planned for it. "Friendly Gorillas" were brought in to help Alex avoid hitting people and to learn more appropriate ways of expressing feelings.

Too often, in traditional treatment approaches, we expect children to change their long-standing behavior patterns just because we intervene or make a placement in a program. Part of the magic of Alex and Shirley's story is that Karl did not have that unrealistic expectation. He prepared for these behaviors, and, with Shirley, created an intervention approach geared toward slowly but surely modifying them. Wraparound interventions rely on this understanding that children with unique troubles will not give up troubling behaviors easily. It is our job to help children understand and meet the needs underlying their behaviors. It is the job of the professional to figure out what drives a child's behavior and to find a way to help the child do better.

---

[1] NAMI-CAN per se has ceased to exist as a separate part of NAMI, which has integrated its child and adolescent focus in with its general program.

Alex's story also teaches a lesson about anticipating behavior. The first question to ask when a child's behavior takes us by surprise is, "Why did we fail to anticipate it?" Karl asked Shirley, "Can you tell when Alex starts to escalate?" When we learn to answer this question about an individual child, we have gained a great tool in helping him or her. Shirley knew the answer, but often, we must help parents and other caregivers discover it. We should not be surprised when children do things that they ordinarily do, just as Karl was not surprised by the fact that Alex hit people. Rather, we need to anticipate these behaviors and prepare for them.

The magic in this story keeps growing for me. Each time I hear it I learn something new, and I have heard it many times. When we learn to discover the strengths in families and their children and help them anticipate their needs, we will need fewer magic wands.

Postscript

Originally, this chapter was titled "Alex's Story," and for years Karl has told the story referring to "Alex and his mother." As we were editing this chapter, however, it dawned on us that both Karl and I had done Alex's mother a great disservice. Not only had we neglected to give her a name—referring to her only as "Alex's mother," but we also continued to present this as Alex's story. So we gave her a name, Shirley, and rewrote this chapter as "Alex and Shirley." Each of us continues to learn!

brenda

A Story About Individual Strengths and Strength-Based Approaches

Does your résumé include the fact that you are cranky when you get up in the morning? Does it admit that when you are under pressure you don't perform as well as you do at other times? Of course not! But don't we do this to young people all of the time? The human service agency is the only place where we create résumés for children and youth that only focus on their weaknesses! That's not very fair, is it?

Brenda first came to Kaleidoscope after being turned away by a number of other agencies due to her history of suicide attempts: by the age of 18, Brenda had tried to kill herself 13 times. This behavior had played a part in her having been in 16 previous placements, including group homes, residential treatment institutions, and hospitals.

At the time she came to Kaleidoscope, she had just been discharged from her last residential placement following her latest suicide gesture. The institution in which she had been living had developed serious questions about what their own risk and liability would be if Brenda were to seriously harm herself, so they chose not to continue to serve her at all. This was not the first time this had happened to her.

Brenda had come into the service system at a very early age, after having conflicts both at home and school. Her mother had asked for help on numerous occasions, but she was not offered the services she would have needed to keep Brenda with her at home. As a result, she was left with little or no help, and Brenda's behavior got worse and worse. At the point when Brenda started to get physically aggressive, she was placed in out-of-home care for the first time—first in a hospital and later at a residential treatment institution. Over time, Brenda began trying to harm herself as well as others. She was labeled over and over again with a multitude of diagnoses. Many different psychotropic medications were prescribed for her, and like many youngsters in our system, she became an accomplished amateur pharmacist. Yet there was little change in her behavior; she continued to abuse herself and others.

Brenda's history did not matter to us at Kaleidoscope. Her high number of suicide attempts did not overwhelm us. It seemed to me that anyone who could make 13 suicide attempts and fail wasn't all that serious about taking her life. So although I agreed that Brenda needed some protection from this scary-looking behavior to protect her from killing herself by accident, I chose not to define who she was based on this one troubling aspect of her life.

The first time I met Brenda, I sat with her and asked her a series of questions that were designed to tell us what she liked to do, whom she liked, and what she was good at. "Have you ever worked with anyone who you really liked and felt comfortable with?," I asked.

She thought for a few moments and finally said, "Yes!" She told me about a psychologist who worked at one of the local hospitals where she had been placed. Brenda felt he had helped her to make more progress than anyone with whom she had worked in the past.

I asked her, "How long did you work with him?"

She replied, "Only six months."

"Why only six months?"

"Well," she said, "I got moved to another residential placement and they said that I couldn't go to him. When I asked why, they said that they had their own therapist and I had to use him."

Unfortunately, this is not an uncommon phenomenon. We often move children from one therapist to another, severing relationships they have developed. Then we wonder why the young people we serve don't trust the therapeutic process.

Next, I asked Brenda, "Is there anything you really like to do or you feel you are good at?"

"I draw good cartoons," she claimed.

I then asked her to show me some of her cartoons, and she reached down into a plastic garbage bag and pulled one out. (If you will allow me to digress from the story for a moment, I would like to point out one of the tragedies of our service system that Brenda's story brings to life. Children and adolescents in our systems move from place to place—which we usually require them to do with great frequency—with all of their meager possessions in what might be called child welfare luggage: garbage bags! And yet we like to talk about the importance of raising their self-esteem.)

When I saw Brenda's cartoons, my impression was that they were not so great. Yet, I saw an opportunity to use her interest and pride in the cartoons as a way to engage her. I told her, "There is a blank wall in our office that is in desperate need of a painting. If you paint me a picture to put up there—a picture describing what the Kaleidoscope family might look like—I will pay you for it."

She was not impressed. She said, "Right, like $10 or $15 or something like that."

"Oh no," I said, "I'm willing to pay you $200!"

"No way!" she exclaimed.

"I'm not putting you on," I replied.

I've hardly ever seen a youngster get quite so excited. Brenda had never even had one hundred dollars of her own and here was a chance to make two hundred. She said, "Okay, I'll do it." I actually think that she saw me as a sucker because she herself didn't really believe in her work.

At the same time Kaleidoscope began to support Brenda's drawing, we found her an apartment a half block away from the hospital where her favorite psychologist worked. We contacted this trusted therapist and got him to agree to provide ongoing therapy for Brenda twice a week and with extra time available for emergencies. Initially, this psychologist was reluctant to take responsibility because he was not sure it was safe for Brenda in the community. One of the reasons we chose an apartment so near the hospital was to help him feel more comfortable. Still, it wasn't enough; we had to provide him with a letter relieving him of responsibility should Brenda harm herself. We responded ourselves by surrounding Brenda with one-on-one staff as a precaution to keep her from hurting herself. We also bought her art supplies so she could start her first commissioned painting.

At the end of one week, the one-on-one staff came to my office suggesting that Brenda would never be successful living on her own. When I asked, "Why?" I was told, "She's just too weird." I didn't understand and asked for an example of what this meant. It was explained to me that the first thing Brenda did when she got up every morning was to make her bed. In addition, if there were just one wrinkle in it, she would tear it apart and remake it. She would sweep the floor twice, clean the kitchen sink, and make sure all of her clothes in the closet were lined up by color.

I was baffled. This didn't seem so weird to me. But then I realized the staff who served her were all very young, and like many of our children, felt that cleaning up after yourself was deviant behavior. Rather than viewing this as weird, I chose to see this behavior as both a strength and a vocational opportunity. The agency found her a job working as a maid in a motel. She sang while she cleaned at home and she sang while she cleaned at the motel. It was something she enjoyed doing. We chose a motel as opposed to a hotel because there were fewer people to deal with; and it was a less intimidating setting, one in which we felt she would be more successful.

Finally, Brenda finished the painting. I took one look at it and was very sorry I had commissioned it because I was now obligated to hang it on the office wall. I got in touch with a friend of the agency who matted and framed art. I told him to spare no expense on framing the picture. True to our instructions, it was returned triple-matted in a beautiful frame and looked a whole lot better. This all cost another $200.

It seemed as though Kaleidoscope's Associate Director, Olivia DelGiudice, had a better eye for art than I did. She was so impressed with the picture that she entered it in an art contest of service providers in Northern Illinois, and to my astonishment, it won third prize. I began to like the picture somewhat better.

The next spring Kaleidoscope had scheduled an open house. I asked Brenda, "Would you allow us to use your painting as the cover for the invitation to the open house?"

She looked at me for a few moments and then answered, "Sure, Karl—for $200!" We had given birth to a capitalist!

The night of the open house, Brenda's picture hung by the front door. For the occasion, we had given her two dozen roses and a long white dress. She was radiant, and stood next to the picture, stopping everyone who came by and explaining to them the inner meanings of her picture with the assurance of Picasso.

Much to our surprise, Brenda's mother and sister showed up at the open house. We had been attempting to locate her mother for months because the system had lost track of her after she moved to the East Coast. We couldn't find her, but she found us.

Brenda's sister was graduating from medical school, and I suspect there were still some ill feelings between the two of them. Although her sister has been very supportive of Brenda in the ensuing years, the first thing she said on that night was, "This is a wonderful place, and if I was crazy, I wouldn't mind being here." All of us who had overheard this remark stopped in our tracks, afraid Brenda would make her fourteenth suicide attempt that night.

But Brenda surprised us all. She took her mother by the hand and showed her the picture and talked about winning third prize in the contest. She talked about her apartment and living on her own and about her job at the motel. Brenda told her mother about the psychologist she saw twice a week and about all the money she had rooked out of me.

Brenda never made another suicide attempt. In truth, the job at the first motel she worked at did not work out; but she found employment at another motel and then another one after that. For the first time in her life, Brenda had become independent. She continued to work and live on her own.

Not long ago, I ran into her psychologist. He said that he still saw Brenda on occasion and was taking her to a Chicago Bulls' basketball game for her birthday. I knew Brenda couldn't afford to pay him his regular rate. I asked him why he still saw her, and he replied, "There are just some things you do regardless of the pay."

I believe Brenda's success had a lot to do with the fact we served her unconditionally, and her treatment, while aimed at meeting her needs, was based on her strengths and the things she felt she did well.

Lessons about Individual Strengths

When Karl tells Brenda's story, he opens with the résumé question, which demonstrates how the system's labels can marginalize young people in our society, especially those young people who have had problems. When Karl first met Brenda, she had a very low sense of self-esteem. She did not think she was a good person, that she was likeable, or that she could do anything. She had failed as a family member, as a student, and as a responsible citizen. All she was good at was hurting herself, and sometimes others. Some of the best professionals and institutions in the nation had found her irreparably broken. For her, making attempts on her life was the only way she could run her life, and for the most part the people she had dealt with agreed with her. She was a "suicide." That's how she had been labeled and treated, and that was how she had come to accept herself.

Karl refused to see her that way. He insisted on seeing her simply as a girl—a girl with competencies. He knew in his heart that unless she began to see herself in a more positive light, she would be doomed to always seeing suicide as an answer. Therefore, Karl's aim was to find some things about Brenda that she could be proud of and that could be used to change her self-image from negative to positive. We call this the strength-based approach. Brenda's story focuses on three basic strengths around which Karl and Kaleidoscope centered their approach to her: one, that she was a good and likable person; two, that she could do something well; and three, that she had positive personal characteristics of which she could take advantage.

Most young people who have lived with trouble see themselves very much like Brenda did—as "screw-ups." This identity is confirmed over and over again when the first question they usually hear from various helping individuals they come across is something like, "How did you screw up this time?" I often fall into this trap myself. Instead, Karl asked her something positive: whether she had ever found anyone with whom she had been able to work.

His first question focused on a most important strength—being able to form a positive relationship with another person and, thus being someone that other people find valuable and likeable. The question itself is probably as important as the answer, which is invariably, "Yes." Somewhere along the line, almost every young person has come across someone with whom they have been able to connect. This was true for Brenda, and her answer helped her feel good about herself and started off her relationship with Karl and Kaleidoscope in a positive way. In addition, by asking that particular strength-based question, Karl began to get the point across that someone along the way had recognized that she was likeable. With her positive answer, she confirmed both to Karl and herself that she could be likeable.

By that time, Brenda had probably gotten the feeling that Karl liked her—not only because of his positive approach, but also because he generally likes the young people with whom he meets, and they can feel it. Young people need to be liked. I guess we all do! Being liked is good for people's self-esteem, and liking them is one of the most important things that one can do when trying to help them. Young people and children can sense if you like them. They know this both from how you approach them and through your words and actions. If your actions don't back up your words, they will soon figure out that you don't really like them, and they will treat you and themselves accordingly. Therefore, if you don't like a particular young person, don't try to work with her. You will most likely do more harm than good. Rather, you should find a person in your agency to work with that youth who likes her.

Unconditional care is a basic principle of Wraparound. Liking children is important if our care is to be unconditional. When our own children do something that we don't like, we don't kick them out or hurt them, because we love them and are committed to them. We find the fortitude to get past the bad times and to learn from these trials. In so doing, our children have the security to be able to learn and grow. When we are helping young people and children who are not our own, it works the same way. It is our caring for them unconditionally that allows them to process the troublesome things they have done and grow past them. In this way, the strength-based approach and unconditional care evolve from the same root: liking and caring for children. (This doesn't mean that we don't get frustrated and angry with them at times, because we certainly do!)

The fact that Brenda figured out quickly that Karl and the people at Kaleidoscope liked young people made her more comfortable with them from the beginning. Later she discovered that Karl and the other staff had become her friends. Karl often describes the young people that he has worked with as his friends. These friendships began as part of the helping process and often continue for many years. Youngsters who have lived with trouble and sadness begin to redefine themselves with positive self-esteem once they feel that they are likable and have become someone's friend. Karl may not have liked or become friends with every child and youth served by Kaleidoscope but someone there did.

In her response to Karl's first question, "Have you ever worked with anyone that you really liked and felt comfortable with?" Brenda demonstrated that she had a good sense of who liked and cared for her. The person that she told Karl about had not only connected with her but had liked her so much that he was willing to work with her gratis when she did not have the money to pay his fees.

A second aspect of the strength-based approach to care demonstrated by Brenda's story is finding something that the youth believes he or she does well or even just likes to do. Karl's next questions for Brenda were about what she did well. She indicated that she was proud of her cartoons. Even though Karl was not impressed with her cartoons, he understood that this was an area where she felt she had some talent. He understood full well that youngsters need adult encouragement whether or not a piece of work is great, or even good. When an infant says a new word, we reward it, no matter how poorly he or she might pronounce it. We smile and cheer, the child smiles and cheers, and then tries again, pronouncing the word slightly better each time. Karl did the same. He didn't say, "That's nice, is there anything else that you are good at?" Rather, his response was to offer her too much money for a painting that he thought was probably going to be as bad as her cartoons. The aspects of themselves that young people see as their strengths are important to them, and we need to encourage them by supporting every positive effort they take. It increases their self-esteem. If we accept their positive impressions of themselves, they will begin to assess themselves positively and be willing to accept suggestions from us as to other things they might be able to do differently or better.

Most teenage boys with whom I have worked say that the thing they do best is play basketball; many of them even feel that they are destined for NBA careers. While the rational side of me wants to point out, "You're only 4'8, and you aren't even on a team!" the strength-based side of me leads me to ask them about their prowess as point guards. In addition, when we play some ball together, I can always make them feel good about their playing ability because, no matter how badly they play, they are always legitimately better than I am. (Karl, whose picture hangs in the National Basketball Hall of Fame, can't get away with that.)

Brenda's use of her art to build her self-esteem didn't emerge all at once; it evolved slowly over a long period of time. Her first reaction was that Karl was a fool—"How can I be that good?"—and she played it for all it was worth. Later, she began to believe that maybe she *could* be that good. When she asked for another $200 to put her picture on the invitation, it was only part manipulation; the rest was the product of a growing feeling that she was valuable as an artist and person. Later, when Brenda's high-achieving sister insulted her, she used her art to demonstrate her newfound feeling of strength and self-esteem.

The third aspect of strength-based thinking in Brenda's story has to do with taking advantage of one's personal characteristics. In this case, we are told about how her neatness led to her job as a motel maid. Here is an example of a different type of strength recognition: the reframing of a perceived deficit as a strength. To a practiced observer, Brenda's bed-making and cleaning activities might appear to be pathological. The Kaleidoscope staff labeled her behaviors as "weird." With my psychiatrist hat on, I might call them "obsessive-compulsive." Either way, when described that way, the characteristic appears to be a symptom of pathology that should be eradicated through some kind of treatment. Karl, on the other hand, saw that particular behavior as representing a strength that could be used to Brenda's advantage. In fact, Karl jokingly points out, when we see excessively messy adolescents, no matter how messy, we accept that behavior as being within the normal range, yet we think of neatness in an adolescent as abnormal.

Karl's approach to Brenda's neatness is a perfect example of how strength-based approaches fit in with another Wraparound principle, that of individualized services. Whether pathological or not, the cleaning was something Brenda liked to do and was good at. It lent itself to a perfect job opportunity—one in which she had a good chance of being successful. Brenda needed a job. Her particular neatness characteristic and love of cleaning made it so that her individualized job choice became obvious. It built on her strength and made success more probable, although as the story goes, not inevitable. The better we become at recognizing an individual's strengths, the easier it becomes to create truly individualized interventions for and with them.

Strengths are not always obvious! When children have spent many years in institutional settings that have focused on their weaknesses, their strengths have a tendency to get lost. At such times, we have to "reach" in order to find strengths, and depending on our individual degree of creativity, some of us have to reach more than others. Brenda's story presents several examples of the need to "reach" in recognizing those strong points that Brenda used to help her get past her problems. Brenda's artistic interests and talents eventually became a basis on which to build part of her new view of herself—even though neither Karl nor Brenda was initially convinced that she was very talented. Now, almost everyone can see it. Her compulsive neatness was a little harder to pick out as a strength. Karl did it quickly, but his staff saw it as a liability. In the story as it appears here, Karl tells you that he saw it as a strength before you had a chance to figure it out for yourself. We each have to ask ourselves, "If I had been there instead of Karl, which way would I have seen that attribute—like Karl or like the Kaleidoscope staff?"

Let's take a short strength-based test. I'll tell you one of my stories. This is about the day I went to visit the Director of Mental Health of one of our states. When I got to his office, he was just getting off the phone. He seemed upset and began to talk about how difficult it was to do his job. His phone call had been about a youth who had run away from a state institution. "Kids do that all the time," he complained, "but this one stole a train!" He then asked for advice as to how to handle this troublesome situation. It seemed to me that he was reacting very much like most of us would in that situation, especially if the child's care was your responsibility.

Was your first reaction to that story, "Wow, what a kid! He stole a train! How many young people do you know could do that without killing himself or others or causing an accident?" If it was, then the next step would be to suggest to the Director that he might find the boy a job with trains. In addition, did you wonder, "What kind of runaway was it?," with the hope of finding a strength there? I usually think that running away from a bad placement has some strength built into it. Sometimes children run away for good reason, or they run to good places. As I look for strengths, I always ask if a runaway episode was a good one or a bad one (in other words, did the youth run to a safe home or to the streets?). A second question I ask is whether the runaway was a competent or an incompetent one (was the youth able to take care of him or herself in a responsible way or did he or she get into trouble or into harm's way?).

If you are concerned that you didn't find the strengths in this exercise, don't worry too much. It's not easy to reframe events and characteristics that you have always seen as problematic, and it can take a great deal of practice. To help you, Karl and I will generally identify the strengths that we have found in the children and families whose stories we tell in other chapters.

Not being able to recognize strengths is not the only problem people face in fully accepting a strength-based approach. Professional attitude and training is another. I've heard Karl tell Brenda's story umpteen times now, and each time, I still ask myself, "Is that the way I would have approached her?" My professional training as a psychiatrist pushes me to worry about suicide attempts. I have a natural tendency to focus on doing something about them, to label the person a "suicide," and to create an intervention plan primarily focused on that particular behavior. Not only is this the way I was trained, but I feel that it is important to protect myself from getting sued for malpractice.

But such an approach had not worked for Brenda in the past. Actually, it seemed to backfire. The more people focused on her suicidal behaviors, the more those behaviors became a problem. The more they labeled her a "suicide," the more she came to believe that that was what she was, and she ran her life based on that image of herself.

On the other hand, Karl understood that if she were going to identify herself based on some personal characteristic, it should be a good part—a strength. "I am an artist" is a better identity than "I am a suicide." I am a "good cleaner" is better than "I am a neat freak." When Karl focused on her strengths, Brenda followed suit and did the same thing for herself.

From a professional point of view, it might seem that focusing on suicide is an important intervention. That is what most people refer to as the medical model, which is based on the philosophy, "Here is something that is broken, let's fix it." In the case of suicide, our interventions are often lifesaving. Yet while that is true, it places the focus of attention on the broken aspect of a person's life. Yes, we must protect people from their suicidal impulses, but if we do not simultaneously help them find a better image of themselves, they will never give up the self-destructive behavior or their identity as a broken or bad person. Conversely, an intervention that focuses on a person's strengths (while at the same time taking pains to protect that person's life) will ultimately begin to shift the focus of the person's own thoughts to his or her positive attributes. That person will then begin to see him or herself as positive person. That is what happened to Brenda.

Karl did not forget that Brenda had a history of trying to kill herself. He tells us that he protected her with one-on-one helpers who not only protected her but also protected him and his agency from liability. At the same time, however, he played down that aspect of her treatment—only doing it because he needed to protect her and not because he saw it as the way to help her get better. In this way, he demonstrates how one can work from a strengths-based perspective while still being clinically responsible.

Fear of manipulation is another barrier to operating as a strength-based helper. Some would describe Karl as a victim of manipulation when he paid $200 for what he considered a bad painting. Even more people would describe him that way after he paid another $200 to use Brenda's picture on the invitation to the open house. Maybe so, but Karl's response was to see this as a new strength, "We had given birth to a capitalist." Manipulation is not a particularly bad trait as long as it is used toward positive outcomes. Brenda's interactions with Karl around the paintings may have some manipulative qualities, but they were not necessarily bad. At the same time,

Karl probably manipulated Brenda as much as he allowed her to manipulate him. Lourie's Law of Manipulation recognizes the positive power in manipulating and of being manipulated when it comes to working with youth (I'm not sure how true it is in other realms). Lourie's Law states, "It is all right to be manipulated as long as the following criteria are met: 1) you know you are being manipulated; 2) the person manipulating you knows that you know; and 3) you get to manipulate back, as long as that manipulation is in the service of helping the child." When one adheres to Lourie's Law, manipulation stops being a dangerous and destructive thing and begins to take its place as a potentially beneficial tool. In Brenda's case, it played a positive role in helping her bolster her newfound self-esteem and survival skills.

A final question one might ask me as we finish the discussion of strength-based approaches, "Do you wear rose-colored glasses?" That is just the accusation I frequently get from an individual with whom I have worked for a while. She says that I don't see the troublesome things that she does, only the good ones—that my strength-based approach is a denial of reality. Each time she confronts me this way, I pause to configure my response. I think to myself, "Yes, I do recognize things she does that are problematic, but should she and I spend our time figuring out what she did wrong—doing a play-by-play analysis of a situation about which she already feels bad and most often embarrassed—or should we be focusing on getting past it so that we can then focus what she is doing that works?" I usually tell her, "No, I'm not wearing rose-colored glasses. I know that you mess up sometimes, but I also know that you are pretty good at analyzing those incidents to death and beating yourself about them. You don't need me to do that too. What can be productive here is to focus on your strengths and the positive aspects of what happened so that you can move on in a positive direction." She doesn't always believe me. She thinks that she is a "screw-up"—that has been part of her identity. I don't see her that way and through my taking a strength-based approach, she is learning that she is really okay and that her identity is as a "good person." Brenda learned that, too.

samuel and ramon

Stories About Creativity, Flexibility, and
Individualized Interventions

Samuel

Several years ago, we at Kaleidoscope were getting ready to expand our services
and move our offices into a new neighborhood in Chicago. We knew it would
be an advantage to our staff and the young people who came to our offices if
the gangs in our new area viewed us positively. In addition, we saw this as an
opportunity to form a relationship with some gang leaders—something we
had been unsuccessful with in the past.

Our plan was simple. We decided not to do social work with our local
gang leaders or to educate them. Rather, we called them in to the office and
asked them if they would be willing to do some consulting work for the agency.
They wanted to know, "What do you want?"

I replied, "I need a demographic study of the community that we are
about to move into."

They asked, "What do you mean?"

I said, simply, "I will pay you to go into this community and secure the
following information. Is it safe for our adolescents to come and go to the
office without gang intimidation, regardless of their gang affiliations, and is
there good transportation for getting to the office?" They agreed to do the
study and told me they would get back to me in a couple of days. I already
knew that transportation was not an issue. What was more important was the
fact they represented the two major rival gangs, and if they wanted to, they
had the power to ensure the safety of the young people coming to our office.

They came back in a couple of days, and told me our people would be
safe and outlined the various transportation lines which could be used. Upon
finishing their oral report, they asked to be reimbursed. I told them they had

done a great job; but that I needed to have their report in writing, otherwise I would not be able to account for their payment. I assured them that, if they were charming, they could dictate their findings to one of our secretaries, who would then be happy to type the report for them. This was my way of creating an opportunity for my staff to spend more time with them to develop a relationship. Of course, this was also a way to help them understand business practice.

They found a secretary to type their report, and frankly, it looked better than some of the clinical reports for which we had paid a lot more money. When they got their money, they told me they liked this consulting work and would be happy to perform any other duties along this line that I could think of and pay for.

A few months later, we moved into our new offices. During the first week of occupancy, the chairman of our board visited us to look at our new space. On leaving, he discovered someone had stolen his car from our parking lot. I was very angry and called up my "consultants" and told them what had happened. I complained there was nothing in their report that talked about the possibility of car theft. They informed me that I had not asked them for such information, and had I done so, they would have been glad to supply the information...for a price.

I saw this need to provide some security for our cars as a grand opportunity. What I was looking for went far beyond merely providing parking protection; it was really aimed at setting up an employment opportunity for one of the gang leaders. We went to the building owner and suggested that we would be willing to hire, train, and supervise security for the parking lot if they would pay the salaries. They agreed that if it were successful, after the first year they would be willing to contract with the security personnel directly for this service.

While working with the gangs, one of the young gang leaders I came to regard highly was Samuel. He claimed to have 250 members working for him in his gang organization. I wasn't sure if that was true, but I did know that, at the age of fifteen, he had the power to order the death of other human beings. Samuel was a nervous young man who suffered from a substance abuse problem. Part of this may well have been related to the fact he had a tremendous amount of stress with his job, especially considering that it was a position from which one doesn't get fired, rather, one gets killed.

Samuel told me he was looking for a way out of his high-stress administrative position. He further went on to let me know that when others had attempted to offer him work in the past, the jobs which had been suggested were menial labor, such as bagging groceries in supermarkets, working in fast-food restaurants, or doing day labor. These were not appealing to Samuel, because Samuel was like a lot of administrators—he preferred to tell people what to do rather than do it himself.

Our approach to Samuel was a little different. We asked him if he would like to own his own business. After some negotiation, he agreed to try it.

Now this situation was not as simple as I sometimes make it sound. For, while Samuel was very bright, he did not have the best work ethic, unfortunately. We feared this problem would keep Samuel from getting the job done and that he would need some form of support. So we teamed him with Kevin, a young person in our services who had a really great work ethic but who could not get things done because he was somewhat limited in other ways.

At Kaleidoscope, we believed you must always individualize the services and interventions to fit the abilities and strengths of the people you serve, but also their interests and limitations. So we hoped that mixing Samuel's strengths and limitations with Kevin's would lead to the creation of a team that worked for both of them.

At first, we were not sure it was going to work. For the first few months it was difficult—at least for me—since this project was my responsibility and I had made the assurance that it would work. Anytime there was a communication breakdown or someone failed to show up, I became the highest paid parking lot attendant in Chicago. But the key intervention I used during this year—when I was not watching cars—was to continually place the responsibility of the parking lot on Samuel and Kevin's shoulders. If there were conflicts and they both complained that they needed to be off at the same time, I would simply respond to them, "How are you going to work it out?" Ultimately, they did. Although I sometimes had to do their work, by the end of the first year, they had established such a successful operation that the building owner felt they were responsible enough that he could work directly with them.

Lessons From Samuel on Individualized Services

If you wanted to have the head of a major corporation, like AT&T, come and work for you, would you offer him or her a job cleaning floors or making hamburgers? Of course not! At best, such an offer would be found ludicrous and amusing, but more likely, it would be taken as an insult, leading to an angry response from the executive. Asking a highly competent person to do such unskilled tasks would be a stupid waste of that person's abilities. Yet, this is what we do to young people all the time. We say to a youth, "Because you are young, the only job you can handle or I should trust you with is an unskilled task." We present an attitude that says, "Go wash the floor and shut up!" or "Why can't you be thankful that I gave you any job at all, even one you think is a lousy one that doesn't use your strengths and abilities?"

This is a fine example of what some people call the "cookie-cutter" approach, a "one-size-fits all" mentality under which we generalize about a youth based on some aspect of their being such as age, sex, race, socioeconomic status, and, most damaging, behavior. Most often when a job is concerned, age is the primary criterion. Many people automatically come to the conclusion that because an individual is a youth, the best or only job for him or her is in a fast-food restaurant, or the like. This would never happen with an adult, with whom one would first go through a process of discovery, weighing the adult's education, experience, and preferences before making a job recommendation.

Jobs are not the only area in which cookie-cutter approaches are used. Such generalizations about people's needs and how to respond to them exist for every aspect of a child's life: schooling, placement, therapy goals, and medications, to mention a few. When we know that an individual has a substance-abuse problem, we automatically make a number of assumptions about what type of person he or she is and the interventions that are most likely to work. The same is true for victims of child abuse and neglect. Unfortunately, this also seems to hold true for such aspects of people's lives such as race, what part of town one lives in, and what kind of behaviors a person has demonstrated.

Not only can the cookie-cutter approach easily become destructive, such as when it takes on a racist quality, but it also just does not work well. One of the things that experience with Wraparound tells us is that when an intervention approach is truly individualized, it works better. I use the term "truly individualized" here because many people think that if they have enough different "cookie-cutters" that they apply to people on an individual basis, they have created an individualized approach. Instead, they have merely created an individualized-*looking* approach.

If he were going to make a meaningful connection with a high-level gang member, Karl knew that it was imperative to come up with an approach that was truly individualized for the person and situation.

He knew that if he used an approach that was not specifically oriented to who and what Samuel was, Samuel would at the very least blow Karl off, and in the worst case maybe even blow him up. Karl understood that he should *not* do two things under any circumstances—insult Samuel and make him angry! Karl saw that Samuel was a high-level gang executive, and to offer him a lesser job could do both.

Most of all, Karl wanted to connect with Samuel, and he knew that the best way for this to happen was to recognize both his strengths and liabilities, and take an individualized approach to using them. And, it worked! To this day, Samuel calls Karl "Dad," and Samuel and Karl consider each other friends. He did this by recognizing that Samuel had both administrative abilities and deficits. He created a job situation for Samuel that used his strengths and brought in a coworker to balance his weaknesses. Karl went so far as to utilize Samuel's role in the community to help Kaleidoscope, an action that not only benefited the program, but also validated Samuel's stature and self-esteem. Samuel's story demonstrates the basic principles of individualized intervention. Before we delve into the details, however, Karl has a second story to share.

Ramon

I got a call from a state official about a young man for whom they were having difficulty finding resources. He was 18 years old, and at that time was under the jurisdiction of the Department of Corrections. Ramon had been suspected of involvement in a murder as well as being affiliated with a gang. I must emphasize, there was really no proof of either of these allegations. I was also told that Ramon was intellectually limited, and therefore, it would be better not to use any humor or to be too subtle when I interviewed him.

Ramon was being detained because he had walked into one of the state's local social service offices and had become enraged because he didn't believe the service was fast enough. Then, he threw a water cooler at the caseworker. Not just the bottle of water on the top, but the whole machine. I took from this that Ramon was evidently very strong.

I first met Ramon at a meeting hosted on his behalf by one of the judges in juvenile court. When I walked in, 22 human service professionals were sitting around a table trying to figure out what could be done with Ramon. Now, before I meet a youth for the first time, I do not like to read all of the information I can get about him or her. I'd rather gather my initial impressions from my meeting with the child. Nevertheless, before I met with Ramon, I was asked to read all of the material which had been accumulated on him. When I read it, two things stood out. One was that Ramon really liked music and dancing. The second was rather frightening: Ramon liked to do push-ups and could do 180 of them without stopping.

As I finished reading the material, the corrections staff brought Ramon in. He was shackled with both hand and ankle cuffs with a chain stretching between the two. He was wearing a T-shirt, and his muscles bulged as if he had been a weightlifter most of his life.

In spite of Ramon's reported intellectual limitations, I found I was able to have a very useful conversation with him in which he not only was able to tell about himself and the things he liked to do, but he also did it in a humorous way. Upon taking a first glance at Ramon I asked, "Wow, you've got a lot of muscle on you! How many push-ups can you do?"

He looked around the small room we were in, and then replied, "One hundred and eighty," and then added, "But I could probably do more, if I wasn't in such a small place." And we both laughed.

When I asked, "What do you like to do?", he said, "Well, I like to work out, and I like to dance."

I refrained about asking him about the murder allegation or about throwing the water cooler. I felt I didn't know him well enough or know enough about him at that point to ask. Also, I didn't want him to throw me. I have never asked him about the murder; that's his business to share with me if and when he wants to. But, now that we know each other and are friends, I do tease him about the water cooler.

After my meeting with Ramon, I suggested to the assembled group that Kaleidoscope should be given an opportunity to provide services for Ramon in the community, and they reluctantly agreed.

When we began to work with Ramon, we were fortunate enough to find treatment foster parents who were not only dedicated, but who also supplemented their income by running a dance troupe on weekends. We thought this would appeal to Ramon.

We then went to a local university to try and secure some one-on-one companions, because we felt it was imperative that Ramon receive around-the-clock support. I explained this to one of the coaches in the athletic department. He said I could choose from a couple of young men who would fit the bill. He asked if I preferred these young men to backgrounds in psychology or sociology. I responded that primarily, they only needed one ability—to be able to do 181 push-ups, one more than Ramon!

When we hired the two young men, they wanted to know exactly what their job was. We told them they would be companions who were to lift weights, run, and do push-ups with Ramon, with the primary purpose of tiring him out, so when he came back to the foster home he would be exhausted. As I mentioned in Chapter 3 (Alex and Shirley's story), at Kaleidoscope we had learned that tired children cause fewer problems. So our goal was to keep Ramon physically active in the evenings with athletics and on the weekends with dancing. We also arranged for Ramon to attend an alternative school, and his two companions were also to accompany him there. We found a therapist to see Ramon on a weekly basis to help him gain better impulse control. Finally, we started to search for any of his relatives who could be found. We were going to take it one day at a time. And to our great relief, Ramon enjoyed the foster home and became friends with his companions with whom he worked out and went to school.

This plan proceeded without incident for about six months. At that point, Ramon came to see me, evidently very upset. He told me that he was tired of having these "jocks" following him around all the time. He said he didn't have a life and if I didn't get rid of the "jocks," it wouldn't make sense for him to live and he would jump out of my sixth-floor window.

As Ramon and I talked, it became evident that his concern had to do with the fact he had become extremely interested in a young lady and felt it was impossible to court her while surrounded by staff. It was then I told Ramon how proud of him I was. Because six months ago, as opposed to threatening to jump out of the window if the plan wasn't changed, he would have threatened to throw me out of the window instead. I said, "Ramon you are attempting to manipulate me. That's wonderful, it's the American way!"

Ramon felt he would be able to continue doing well without the "jock" companions. So we made adjustments in the plan to accommodate Ramon's romance, and Ramon was able to successfully stay in the community.

Had we had a choice and had not been committed to an unconditional care philosophy, I don't believe we would have tried to work with Ramon in the community. Had we not had an individualized approach, our plan would not have been successful. We were as surprised as anyone else that Ramon's plan worked, but I think it worked because we based the plan on Ramon's strengths and interests and we were committed to serving him.

Lessons from Ramon on Individualized Services

To me, the four most important words in Ramon's story are when Karl says, *"Two things stood out."* Karl's whole approach was based on two facts that might otherwise have been overlooked. He did not focus on Ramon's outrageous history of behavior or on his destructiveness or his supposed intellectual limitations. He focused instead on two facts: *"Ramon really liked music and dancing,"* and *"Ramon liked to do push-ups and could do 180 of them without stopping."* Around these two pieces of information, an intervention approach was individualized— based on Ramon's strengths.

In a more traditional approach, any intervention planning would have been centered around the fact that Ramon had been violent, had a tendency to easily lose control, and was intellectually compromised. A plan would have focused on these issues and would have attempted to ameliorate them. But with Ramon, and many children and adolescents who have unique problems, those plans do not work. By focusing on weaknesses, we often only highlight them and make them more obvious and more of a problem. Rather, Karl chose to approach Ramon from the standpoint of his strengths.

Given Ramon's history, finding strengths was not easy to do. Karl found two. The first of these was easy to deal with—liking music and dancing. Traditionally, although most of us would agree that these are strengths, they are not always viewed in a positive light. Adults often dislike the music that young people prefer or the dances they most enjoy. Karl, however, saw them as the most obvious of Ramon's strengths and felt they needed to be major parts of the intervention. He did not do this by more traditional means like buying him a tape player, getting him music lessons or making sure that he attended dances at school. These interventions would not have worked for Ramon; he was out of control, and there is a good chance that he would have thrown the tape player at someone and/or disrupted the dance.

Karl found a more creative way to utilize these strengths in a manner that had the potential for a greater impact while at the same time meeting Ramon's individual needs. He placed Ramon with foster parents who loved music and dancing—they ran a Latin dance troupe in their spare time. Now, I do not think that Karl necessarily thought that Ramon would join a dance troupe. The real genius in this placement is that the family loved music and dancing so much that they could see Ramon's interest as something wonderful—and saw him, therefore, as a good person. Ramon, in turn, immediately felt accepted in the home and began to feel good about himself for the first time in many years. Ultimately, he did practice dance with the troupe. Karl told me once that when he went to visit Ramon and his foster family, he would walk in and find them all dancing together. As they danced, they were involved in a mutual give-and-take about the dance steps—how they were working and how they could be improved. This piece of the intervention for Ramon was truly individualized around using a strength to help offset a problem.

The second area of strength that Karl recognized was Ramon's physical abilities. For most of Ramon's life, people had seen his physical strength as a liability. After all, he had used that power aggressively, and it had been a major factor in his constant troubles and ultimate placements. It even frightened Karl! By this point, however, you should have no trouble seeing how Karl came to the conclusion that a violent child who was strong enough to do one hundred and eighty push-ups can be seen as a strength. Even so, if you have some trouble seeing this as a strength, you are not alone. Most people in the children's services fields would be equally as scared of Ramon's physical strength and his potential for violence, and either ignore it, hoping it would go away, or focus on corralling it through some form of restraint.

Those who could agree that Ramon's physical strength was of great value to him see that attribute as the underpinning of his self-esteem and understand that a truly individualized intervention approach will find a way to make it part of his recovery. Karl did. Of all the things that Ramon liked to do, physical training was the thing he liked to do best. He was proud of his body and its abilities. Karl wanted him to do things that made him proud. Karl also wanted to keep him busy doing something nondestructive. Remember Karl's belief: *"If you keep children physically worn out, they won't have energy left with which to get into trouble."* So, the plan for Ramon included a bodybuilding program, through which he focused on his body as a strength and which dissipated most of his energy on a positive pursuit.

Although the primary focus of Karl's individualized plan for Ramon centered on these two basic strengths, Karl understood that the plan also had to address Ramon's liabilities. He knew that Ramon needed to be protected from his own anger and volatility, and that the community needed to be protected from Ramon. The answer was companions, or "one-on-one" aides. This type of helper is probably the most common form of nontraditional intervention used today in the field of child mental health, and on the surface, the use of this type of aide with Ramon does not appear very innovative or individualized. Karl uses "one-on-ones" for very special, individualized purposes, however. As Karl mentioned, they used to be called "Friendly Gorillas." This name specifies two specific purposes: 1) being a friend when one is needed; and 2) having the capacity to control situations when they occur. Ramon needed both. But this was not the whole story when it came to individualizing the companions' use with him. Karl, recognizing Ramon's greatest liability, demanded that the companions have one vital skill—to be stronger than Ramon—along with all the other criteria that make a good aide. Protection was not the only purpose for the companions, however. Their presence was intended to address the strength aspects of Ramon's physical abilities. Karl went to the coach to find the companions because he felt this was the best way to find individuals with a teachable knowledge of strength training. In these ways, Ramon's companions were not just one-on-one aides; they represented a position which was individually conceived based on Ramon's strengths and needs.

Another major facet of individualized services is the need for them to be flexible. When Ramon negotiated with Karl to have his companion support changed so that he could go out on dates, Karl was able to comply. This is not an unusual situation in the world of children's services; almost anyone can stop a service after it starts. But stopping the service was not the issue. Often service providers and families are unwilling to give up a valuable service like a one-on-one aide for a combination of reasons. First, these services are often hard to obtain in the first place. Second, if you stop them even for a short time, and you ultimately find they are necessary, that service will be gone, and resumption of the service will be as difficult to obtain as it was originally. For these reasons, if a child wants to try and operate without the one-on-one aide, parents and providers may be unwilling to let them try. Because Kaleidoscope truly believed in individualized services, it created a flexible service provision, in which a service can be stopped and started again if necessary without any trouble at all. Wraparound services rely on this type of flexibility so that services can be individualized on a moment-to-moment basis.

When Karl tells Ramon's story he says, "Had we had a choice and had we not been committed to an unconditional care philosophy, I don't believe that we would have tried to work with Ramon in the community."

Why is an unconditional care philosophy so important in promoting individualized services? Karl gives us an explanation. Everybody wants to be successful, and programs take those children with whom they feel they can be most successful. Unfortunately, there are lots of children to go around, and programs can fill up with the most promising children. This leads to trouble for those children whose problems are unique, severe, and/or have been shown to be difficult to treat. These children often end up in out-of-state or out-of-community residential placements. If a child's problems are unique enough, such as Alex's in Chapter 3, even these highly structured programs, including jails, cannot or do not want to serve him or her.

I'm not even sure that this happens on a conscious level. Some years ago, I worked as Medical Director of a residential treatment center called the Regional Institute for Children and Adolescents - Rockville, Maryland, or RICA-Rockville. I thought that this was a really good program. It was family-oriented and community-based, and it had an even larger day program integrated with the residential program. After the program had been running for a while, we all began to understand who did well in our program and who did not. Those who did best were referred to as "RICA kids." We began to feel that if our program only had "RICA kids" in it, we could really be successful. Why would we want any other kind of kid? After all, there were enough children who were "RICA kids" to keep the place full. While we had no specific policy that excluded other kinds of children and we did not seek out a specific kind of child, we seemed to have a greater and greater percentage of "RICA kids" in the program over time. Had Alex, Samuel, or Ramon been presented to us, we most likely would have made it known that they were inappropriate for the program and would probably do better somewhere else.

As a result, we really did not have to truly individualize our services at RICA, and over time our program became a more and more categorical one. We did not need anything else other than a cookie-cutter approach. If children did not get better in the program, we simply said, "Oh, he (or she) is not a 'RICA Kid!'" If our program had been unconditional, we could not have gotten away with that, and we would have had to find a way to make things work. And the only way to make it work is with truly individualized services.

What I have come to understand over the years is that, unless services are approached in an individualized manner, we cannot make it with children who do not fit a categorical model. They need a Wraparound approach. And, unless we operate under an unconditional care philosophy, it is difficult to force ourselves out of categorical thinking and to create truly individualized interventions.

Lessons on Creative and Flexible Thinking in Wraparound

When I hear Karl's stories of Samuel and Ramon, I marvel about how creative Karl has been in the development of individualized approaches for them. Some of this, of course, has to do with Karl and how special he is in his understanding of the community and individual children and their families. On the other hand, some of it has to do with Karl's ability and desire to think creatively. While some of this creativity is innate, some is the result of a desire to do things differently if they make sense. Not everyone can be as innately creative as Karl (he would even point out that some are more innately creative than he is), but anybody can push themselves to think differently—to think "outside the box," so to say. Thinking outside the box is an art that is essential in developing individualized interventions for children, and it can be learned. To create a business executive out of Samuel, the gang leader, makes sense, but it is not in the realm of conventional thinking, which probably would have seen Samuel's ultimate occupation as making license plates. To seek Ramon's salvation in body conditioning is also unconventional thinking, as most of us would rather have had Ramon's physical strength diminished. To create these solutions ourselves, all we have to do is recognize a child's strengths and needs and search for ideas that will support those strengths, even though they might seem to defy popular wisdom. We can make this work, because we are also identifying the child's needs—even some needs that are created by our outside-the-box ideas to support their strengths—and creating ways to support them. When we push ourselves to think differently, we can be much more creative than when we stick to categorical, cookie-cutter approaches.

Samuel and Ramon both benefited from Wraparound because the approach to their care was individualized. This approach recognized their strengths and other positive aspects of their lives and created interactions that maximized them, while simultaneously recognizing their needs and other barriers to success and working to overcome them. Flexibility and creativity allowed these interventions to be truly individualized and demonstrate the heart of Wraparound intervention.

larry and marcus

Stories About Unconditional Care

Larry

Larry came to Kaleidoscope at age 18, after having been hospitalized for emotional issues for a number of years. In addition to Larry's emotional issues, he was legally blind. He was a frail young man who was so shy that one might call him a recluse. During our first meeting with Larry, however, we quickly realized this was not the full picture: Larry was very bright and had a keen sense of humor. Part of our evaluation included holding up three fingers in front of his face, about five inches from his glasses, and asking him how many fingers he could see. Larry responded, "I can see three fingers." Based on this, we were confident Larry could make it in Kaleidoscope's Independent Living Services. It was our intent to place him in his own apartment and to wrap services around him.

As a rule, Kaleidoscope only places one adolescent in an apartment or in any one apartment building. A lot of the young adults we serve have been through many placements and have spent a large portion of their lives in institutions and residential programs, a situation which has not allowed them to learn how to participate with a roommate or in a family system. As a result, they need to learn independent-living skills, such as taking public transportation, cooking, shopping, doing laundry, and budgeting. We want to be able to prepare them for their worst-case scenario, which in our opinion, is having to live by themselves.

In Larry's case, we made an exception by placing him in an apartment next door to one of our other young people who was also in an independent-living situation. Charles was one of the warmest, most caring people Kaleidoscope had ever served; however, he was intellectually limited. By placing them together, it was our hope that they would partner up: Larry would do the thinking and Charles would become Larry's eyes, arms, and legs.

Charles was very successful in getting Larry out of his apartment and into the community. He also taught Larry how to use public transportation, do shopping and laundry, and myriad other tasks that Larry had not learned while he was institutionalized. This partnership worked beyond our wildest expectations, as we watched each of them grow from their ability to help another person.

One night, however, I received a call from the staff person who had the 24-hour crisis intervention responsibilities for the night. I was informed that Larry had been arrested and was in jail. The on-call person wanted to know whether I would go to the courthouse in the morning to secure Larry's release. I asked for the particulars of his arrest; the staff member told me all would be made clear to me once I got to the courthouse.

The next morning, shortly after arriving at the courthouse, I was allowed to visit with Larry. He was sitting alone in a cell with a great look of dejection on his face. I asked, "What are you doing in here?"

He replied, "You're just not going to believe this one, Karl."

"Okay, tell me the story," I said. It seemed that on the previous afternoon, Larry and Charles had decided to walk to the store and pick up some donuts. Upon leaving their apartment building, Charles noticed a woman across the street trying to get her car out of the snow, where it was stuck. Both Charles and Larry agreed she needed their help. So they got behind her car and started to push it. This was not working. The woman soon suggested that the smallest person should be the one to sit behind the wheel while the other two pushed the car. This turned out to be Larry, and he was instructed that all he had to do, once the car was free from the snow, was to step on the brake—eyesight not being necessary for him to accomplish this.

They finally got the car out into the street. Larry told me it was at this point he realized this would probably be his only opportunity to ever drive a car. So instead of stepping on the brake, he stepped on the gas pedal and careened down the street, hitting five cars.

On this morning, it was my duty to convince the authorities we would make sure that Larry would never drive another car. In my mind I knew this was workable, because, being legally blind, no one would ever give Larry a driver's license.

None of us could have conceived that this young man, who was legally blind and a recluse, would ever have attempted to drive an automobile. And, if someone would have bet me $10 on the first day I met Larry that this was possible, I would have bet a year's salary against their $10. There are many Larrys in this world who are not given the opportunity to raise their potential and who are kept in restricted settings. Everyone deserves a chance to prove what he or she can do, and Kaleidoscope's philosophy of unconditional care and "no reject" policy allowed Larry to explore and expand his capabilities.

Marcus

Marcus challenged Kaleidoscope's commitment to its unconditional care philosophy more than anyone we encountered. He was a young man who had grown up in the Illinois child welfare system. He had been orphaned as an infant, and like a lot of children who are cared for in child welfare systems, he had been moved from placement to placement and from service to service. In one of these many placements, he had been sexually abused. By the time I met Marcus, it was my opinion the system that had taken responsibility for his care certainly had not done the best job in protecting and serving him. This was not the fault of any particular individual; in fact, for the most part they tried to do their best. Our systems don't always work well, however, and what happened to Marcus just sometimes happens.

In one of our first contacts with Marcus, we suggested to him that Kaleidoscope would be his last placement. We impressed upon him that our commitment to him would be the same as our commitment to our own children—and we would continue to serve him regardless of his behavior and whatever occurred. At first, this went very well, because we were able to find Marcus a nice treatment foster home with both a male and a female figure who worked extremely well together, and there were other children in the home. At last, Marcus had a real family. The foster mother was a wonderfully loving and caring lady. Indeed, she took on the role of mother to many of us. I remember the times she came to the Kaleidoscope office at lunchtime to bring me a sandwich, so that, she said, "you will have the energy to work all those long hours you are working."

Unfortunately, as the result of a tragic event, this did not last long. One day while driving to the office, Marcus's foster mother was killed in a car accident. Suddenly, most of the good things that had happened to Marcus over the past year started to come apart. You see, Marcus' experience had been that when something like this tragedy happened, he would be moved out of his foster home. He worried that he would be moved to another placement, and he was tired of starting in new schools and having to make relationships with all new people.

In addition to his feelings about being moved, Marcus had heard us say over and over again that our commitment to him was unconditional, and he did not believe we would live up to it. So he put our philosophy to an unbelievable test. One morning, shortly after the death of his foster mother, I got a call from a Kaleidoscope staff member who told me to make sure I wore jeans when I came into the office that day, because there had been a fire there. By the time I got there, it was clear that it had been a bad fire, and the office was in really poor shape.

In the time immediately following the fire, Marcus continually asked to talk with me. Each time, he told me how horrible it was that we had had this fire. After a week or so, in one of these talks, Marcus finally admitted to me what we had already begun to suspect: he was the one who had set the fire. I firmly believe, if you wait long enough and have enough patience and if you give them a chance, young people will tell you everything. You have to have enough patience to let them get ready to do this, however. In this particular case, we did not have to wait long. We felt Marcus started the fire because he wanted to test whether our commitment to unconditional care was firm. In the years since, I've often told Marcus that if he wanted to give us a test, he and I could have put our heads together and come up with a better test than burning down our office, but that's what he chose to do and that's what we had to work with.

It was our opinion that, as hostile an act as setting the fire was, the system had been more hostile to Marcus by moving him from placement to placement and putting him in a position where he always felt his security was threatened. We understood why he had done what he had, and we forgave him. Then we needed to convince everyone else involved to forgive him also. We talked the child welfare people, the fire department, and the police department into allowing us to continue to provide services to Marcus, which we did.

I always like to tease people in the system about Marcus, because he later became the director of a group home in another state. I will never tell anyone what state he's in, but somewhere in the country there's someone running a group home for young people, who, as one himself, almost completely burned down my office. I do like to give people just one hint to help them to find Marcus to see if he's in their community: for years I've been trying to talk Marcus into taking firesetters into his group home, and he won't do it. I don't know why.

Lessons from Larry and Marcus on Unconditional Care

"No Reject! No Eject!" This is Karl's mantra as he teaches about unconditional care. Karl impresses on us that unconditional care is vital when working with those children who have struggled in our service system for many years. We know that if these children and youth had had the opportunity of receiving unconditional care earlier in their lives, many would never have needed services as intense as either residential treatment or Wraparound. The stories of Larry and Marcus teach us about the two sides of unconditional care: Larry was not rejected by an independent living program just because he was blind, and Marcus was not ejected from Kaleidoscope in spite of the fact that he had burned down their building.

In Marcus' story, Karl says, "Our commitment to him was the same as our commitment to our own children." This is a basic principle of unconditional care. Children in our public service systems are traditionally treated as patients, not children. This would be all right if we were treating a cold or another minor illness, but we are not. We have taken over their lives, we have accepted a parental role—and then we let them down. When parents abandon a child because the going gets tough, we most often punish them by taking away their other children. On the other hand, when agencies or individual helpers abandon a child by giving up on them and kicking them out, we reward them by giving them more children. As a society, we accept the principle that children need consistent, loving, and available parenting, yet when we professionals accept that parenting role, we forget. When a child's behavior is too tough for a program to handle, the child is discharged to a "more appropriate placement." As we saw in Chapter 3 with Alex and Shirley, some youth even get kicked out of jail! Now, I'm sure that Alex didn't mind getting out of jail, but he did mind having to leave home in the first place, as well as all his various, often nice, placements along the way to jail. Children need a home, or at least a home base. They need adults in their lives who are consistent and who see them as valuable enough to stick with them through thick and thin. If we treat children as if they were expendable, that is how they will begin to see themselves. On the other hand, if we let children know that we are helpers for them and their families for the long haul, that we will let them rely on us no matter what the circumstances, and no matter what they do, they will begin to reestablish a sense of positive self-worth.

As children and youth develop, they use their home base as a platform from which they stray in order to explore the world. The behavior of the toddler provides us with a picture of what this looks like in its simplest form. Think of the last time you saw toddlers of 2 or 3 years of age playing on a playground. When they first get there, they hang on for dear life to the parent with whom they came (in this case let's say it's Mom). Then, slowly but surely, they begin to wander away, a short distance at first, and then further and further away. As they move away from their mother, however, they are always looking back to make sure she is still there. After they have wandered for the proper time or distance of the day, they come back to remake their connections with Mom. Going and coming, each time venturing away with the comfort of knowing that Mom will be there when they return. If Mom is not available for them—if the base from which they wander to explore the world is unsure or unstable—they react by either being reluctant to wander at all or by giving up hope of ever finding a solid base and useful relationships.

This scenario of children exploring the world and then coming home to touch base, continues throughout all of childhood, through the teenage years, and into young adulthood. Whenever it is disrupted, children and youth suffer the consequences. Children who spend a part of their lives in out-of-home placements lose their homes on a regular basis. It is a cruel joke that we play on them. First, we introduce them into nice places with nice people, we encourage them to like them and depend on them—and it works. Many foster children go on to call their surrogate parents "Mom" and "Dad"—even when they are not encouraged to do so. Then, when the chips are down, the family or institution says, "Goodbye!" Most children get the real message—"Get lost!"—and take it to heart. After this happens repeatedly, as Karl pointed out in the story, children and youth begin to give up. They lose faith that there will ever be a solid base for them and they learn to mistrust those friendly adults who say, "Trust in me, I'm here to help you."

Along with their faith, children and youth in our systems lose their self-esteem. Each time someone gives up on a child or youth, his or her self-esteem takes another blow. When they perceive "Get lost!" and—as Karl tells us, pack their things in garbage bags—it cuts them to the bone. An unconditional approach allows children and youth to begin to rebuild their self-esteem and to feel valued again.

While they are struggling to find a solid base from which they can rebuild their self-esteem, explore the world, and develop into healthy adults, young people learn to test the commitment of those who promise to help them. This is often as simple as breaking a minor rule. Later, things they do may escalate into seriously troubling behaviors—for example, Marcus burned down the office. Only as the adults in their lives pass tests of increasing difficulty can the most severely troubled youngsters begin to trust that these adults really care more about *who they are* rather than *what they do*.

The cure for this is unconditional care. The child will not get rejected or ejected because of what he has done before he got there or what he does after he gets there. Every one of the young people whose stories appear in this book has learned over time that Kaleidoscope would not give up on him or her—that the organization would uphold its commitment to be a solid base for each child. From this base, each of them has learned that he or she is valued and that it is safe to explore the world and the process of maturing.

Larry's story demonstrates the principle of No Reject. Regardless of whether or not Larry was blind, Karl welcomed him into Kaleidoscope's independent living program. While working on a"No Reject"basis does not ensure unconditional care, it sets an important tone. Karl's philosophy is that, in general, parents do not choose their children. They take what God gives them. Thus, the foster parents in Kaleidoscope's Therapeutic Foster Care environment were not given the power of refusal over which youth they would take into their home. To make this type of open commitment work, the families and staff need to have the understanding that the services required to keep the child in that home or other environment will be there for them—they rely on the promise of Wraparound.

Karl's unconditional approach to Larry began with his initial decision not to reject him from Kaleidoscope just because he was blind. Furthermore, he made an early assessment that someone Larry's age from a similar background and experience would be best served in an independent living environment. While most would be skeptical about a legally blind, formerly institutionalized youth's ability to survive in that type of living situation, Larry was not excluded from that service. Then, in order to serve some bureaucratic need, Karl created a vision test that even Larry could pass.

This was the easy part. To make it possible for Kaleidoscope to unconditionally help Larry thrive in independent living, Kaleidoscope then had to rely on other aspects of the Wraparound principles. They needed to be strength-based, flexible, and creative.

As Karl stated in the story, the Kaleidoscope practice was to have only one young person living in an apartment and apartment building. Never having been trained to live independently as a blind person, it would have been impossible for Larry to live completely alone. Many programs would have rejected Larry on that basis and referred him to a group or alternative family living situation instead. Kaleidoscope, recognizing that independent living was the environment that best met Larry's needs, found a way to make it happen through flexibility. The organization broke its own rule.

It was Kaleidoscope's creativity and strength-based orientation that really made it work for Larry, however. They realized that Larry's strengths lay in his intellect and his ability to relate to and communicate with others. To help him overcome the obstacle of his blindness, he was placed in an apartment next to another Kaleidoscope youth, Charles, who could act as his eyes. Larry was not only blind, but also small and frail and often needed someone to offer him support in physical things he could not do. Charles, on the other hand, needed Larry's intellectual support. Charles would help Larry navigate and get certain physical tasks done, and Larry would help Charles think things through—two young people borrowing strengths from each other. The result was famous for its success; both Larry and Charles flourished in their joint relationship. While Larry never did see any better, through his relationship with Charles he was able to learn to negotiate the world while still living in an age-appropriate environment. Charles was able to learn from Larry how to think things through better and to survive in an adult world.

Although the story about Larry's driving is cute and certainly grabs our attention, the real lesson from his story is in the beginning, when he was accepted into Kaleidoscope in spite of his physical limitations. The lesson to take from the driving incident is that without an unconditional approach it never would have happened at all. Larry would have been languishing in an institutional setting rather than living on his own and being able to experience life to its fullest.

Marcus' story demonstrates the other principle of unconditional care: No Eject. Karl uses it to demonstrate the principle of unconditional care because fire-setting is one of the things that will automatically get a young person thrown out of most settings and prevent him or her from being accepted at others. Another child served by Kaleidoscope was taken out of her home only when she accidentally set a fire, even though she had been abused. She did not return to a home until she was given her own apartment by Kaleidoscope. Marcus, on the other hand, purposely set a fire that destroyed Kaleidoscope's office and he was not ejected.

For parents, keeping children and adolescents even when they do bad, sometimes terrible, things is simple—not only do we love them, we have to keep them. As agencies and individual helpers, it is not so easy. To overcome the incentives our system offers to send these youngsters somewhere else, we need to completely accept the philosophy of unconditional care. I was taught what I have come to think is the underlying tenet of this philosophy before I even heard the term Wraparound.

I was working at the time at the National Institute of Mental Health, and I was asked by the State of North Carolina to help with a problem the state was having in one of its hospital programs. While on my visit to the Raleigh-Durham area, I was given the opportunity to visit part of the Willie M. program. This was the program in which the term "Wraparound" was first used. Willie M. was a youngster who represented a class of adolescents who were mentally retarded, mentally ill, and demonstrating aggressive behaviors. A lawsuit was brought against the state on behalf of Willie and the others in this class of youngsters because they were not receiving appropriate services. The state settled the lawsuit, and in response, created a system in which youngsters included in the class would be placed in one of a number of services available in their community. To make it possible for them to remain in these community-based programs, additional, individually determined services would be added, or wrapped around them.

At times even in this community-based, Wraparound system of services, a youngster needed to spend some time in one of two residential treatment centers that were part of the Willie M. program. These centers were based on the Wraparound philosophy, including an unconditional care component.[1] At that time, I had just ended a stint as Medical Director of a residential treatment center in Maryland. While there, I had been concerned about how children and adolescents who were having a tantrum were restrained. So when I had the chance to visit this model residential program that was part of a Wraparound system, I took the opportunity to learn something. I asked, "What do you do when kids go off?"

For the 20 or so years since then, I have been asking audiences what they think the response I got to my question was. Nobody has ever gotten it right. It was so surprising to me that even I had a hard time processing it at first. They answered, "We have a meeting!"

I said, "What do mean, you have a meeting? How can you do that when you have a kid going off?"

They then gave me an explanation that to me has come to define the crux of the "No Eject" component of unconditional care. "We hold a meeting to figure out how *we* failed to meet that child's need." Of course, they did do something about the child's behavior first, but when things settled down, they did have a meeting in which they asked that question.

Children come to us with behaviors that are at times problematic. We know this when they first enter our care. We should not be surprised by those behaviors. Rather, we need to anticipate them and come up with a plan for how we are going to try to help children avoid them in the future and how we are going to react when they happen. If we are unsuccessful in either, the Willie M. philosophy tells us that it was our fault—not the child's. We know they do those things; they have been doing those things for a long time, and it is *our* job to find a way to help them stop doing them. If we cannot help them stop, then we must find another approach. Traditionally, we have not done that; instead we blame children for being how they have always been, and then we give up on them and kick them out.

To truly accept the unconditional care principle of Wraparound, one must accept the following philosophy: *if a child or adolescent under my care is not doing well, it is because my approach is not working, and I must come up with a better way of working with that youngster.* Turning this philosophy into practice is not an easy proposition, but it can get

---

[1] The fact that Karl and others object to residential services being included as part of a Wraparound services array is discussed in the chapter about Desmond and Tori. For the purpose of this story, however, the fact that this was a residential treatment center does not really matter.

easier if one commits to being nonjudgmental about and accepting of behaviors, to understanding the behaviors' antecedents, and having realistic expectations of children's responses to our interventions. Marcus' story demonstrates most of these characteristics of care.

As Karl tells Marcus' story, he explains how the tragic death of Marcus' new foster mother was directly connected to a decrease in Marcus' ability to control his behavior. Karl understood that Marcus had found a new home and had invested himself in bonding with the foster parent, and that losing that parent was a significant loss to him. He was sure to have a reaction, and that reaction would most likely be reflected by a behavior similar to one he had demonstrated before. Helping individuals are trained to make such connections, and it is not so difficult for most of us to understand what events in people's lives precipitate troublesome reactions. This represents an understanding of the antecedents of behaviors.

Karl went a step further. He recognized that while Marcus' reaction was based in part on the loss of his foster mother, there was also another major factor. Karl had promised unconditional care, and he had not been able to come through for Marcus. While one might say that Karl and Kaleidoscope had not failed to keep their promise, Karl understood that to Marcus unconditional care meant staying in one home. As such, Karl had an understanding and acceptance of the fact that he was not able to keep his promise as Marcus saw it and that was a part of the problem. This is the part of unconditional care that most of us are not so ready to accept, and yet it reflects the underlying unconditional care principle of the helper taking responsibility for his or her part of a youth's behavior.

Furthermore, Karl understood that Marcus' behavior was not only a reaction in part to Karl's promise, it was also a test of Karl's true commitment to unconditional care. Marcus was most likely unaware of this test he was creating, yet Karl could see it, and he accepted the fact that Marcus needed such a test. The system had always let him down; it had always failed earlier tests of its unconditional promises. He needed to test again, and this time he got a different response than he was used to: Karl passed the test.

Karl went still another step further. He did not judge Marcus' worth as a human being based on this one behavior. Having understood the nature of the promise he had made to Marcus, the traumatic manner in which that promise appeared to be broken, and Marcus' need to test, he also anticipated what Marcus' reaction would be—a troublesome behavior. Given his history, no one could have anticipated that Marcus would burn down the building, but given his history, everyone should have anticipated a hostile reaction of some kind. Karl's nonjudgmental approach to what Marcus did even went so far as to accuse the system of teaching Marcus how to react in a hostile manner by being hostile to him through "moving him from placement to placement and putting him in a position where he felt threatened." He recognized that Marcus had learned over the years to react in hostile ways when his world fell apart and his security was threatened. He goes on to tell us that Marcus' reaction to the situation was to be expected, and while not excusable, it created a need to prove Kaleidoscope's commitment to unconditional care rather than kicking Marcus out—the response that Marcus had previously learned to expect from his behaviors.

To pass Marcus' test of Karl's unconditional care philosophy and practice, Karl also needed to become Marcus' advocate. He had to convince others in the community, Marcus' child welfare worker, guardian, the police department, and the fire department, that it was safe to allow Marcus to remain in the community with Kaleidoscope. For this to happen, Karl had to tap the final lesson of unconditional care—adequate and available resources. Karl had to demonstrate to all those around him that the appropriate services could be wrapped around Marcus to the degree that he would no longer be a threat to the community or to himself. Although the story does not detail what services Kaleidoscope provided to Marcus after the fire, Kaleidoscope developed a plan of action based on the input of those who knew Marcus best, including Marcus himself, which addressed how his strengths and other resources could be used to support his needs.

Accepting an unconditional care philosophy and applying it in our professional lives by itself is not an easy shift. Karl ends his story about Marcus by talking about how hard this is. He tells us that Marcus himself will not fully commit himself to the unconditional care philosophy that ultimately was so helpful to him and does not accept firesetters in his group home. Karl says, "I don't know why." I suspect he does know and just does not want to say it out loud: some people may never be able to take the risks inherent in an unconditional approach. There are personal risks: an unconditional commitment to a child or youth means accepting a parent-like role. This most often comes with an emotional attachment, which itself carries some emotional risk. Marcus' story tells us that you also must take the risk that your house will be burned down. There are professional risks: an unconditional commitment means being liable for acts committed by a child for whom you have advocated. Karl told child welfare, police, and fire departments that he could prevent Marcus from burning down anything else and he knew that he would take some of the blame if it happened. Karl was willing to take both the personal and professional risks to keep a firesetter in his program. Marcus is not. How about you?

Larry and Marcus' stories together not only provide a good lesson in the principles of unconditional care and the No Reject/No Eject policy but also demonstrate how all of the basic principles of Wraparound work together. These stories tell us that it is impossible to uphold the promise of unconditional care unless we are strengths-based in our approach; create flexible, creative, uniquely individualized intervention plans; and are community-based in our practice. Furthermore, without the community's support of the Wraparound approach, an active team of committed individuals working together with both Larry and Marcus, and resources to ensure that the needed supports and services could be made available, neither youth's plan could have been enacted.

desmond and tori

Stories About Community-Based Care

Desmond

Although the rest of the world does not necessarily agree, at Kaleidoscope, we didn't believe in residential care. We also didn't believe in institutionalization. The reason we felt this way is that you can't help people learn to live in their own communities by sending them away from home, no matter how nice the residential facility or institution is.

Desmond was one of the young people for whom Kaleidoscope provided services. At age 13, he was living in a poor environment, one of the most notorious housing projects in Chicago. He was living in a family that was not doing the best job of protecting him or keeping him or their home clean, and he was getting into trouble. His mother was constantly being called to school to take him home. A very well-meaning social worker decided this was not good, and maybe even dangerous for him. Because Desmond was very charming and very bright, his caseworker decided she was going to save him by getting him away from his family and out of the projects.

As a result, Desmond was sent to a wonderful institution in northern Illinois—a residential program with a very good reputation in an upper middle-class community. (Even I think that particular institution did good work.) While there, he began to do better, attended a suburban high school, and in the end, graduated in the top 25% of his class.

Everyone was very proud of Desmond, but because he had reached the age of 18 and finished school, his access to public services came to an end. and independent living became his goal. Desmond needed an independent living environment in which he could learn how to live on his own. The city child welfare agency, which had placed him in a suburban community, would not support an independent living program there, so although Desmond had learned to use the resources of an easy-to-live-in community and had developed friends there, he had to return to the city. After all, it was his "home," and the agency thought it was the only place he could go. Unfortunately, it was like taking a child from the Iowa cornfields and sticking him in the inner city. Desmond had lost the sense of what it was like to live in a city, and with it, all of his survival skills. For example, he had forgotten that if you wore your hat on the wrong side of your head in certain neighborhoods, you might get killed. In spite of these problems, what he did have going for him was that he was 6'2 and weighed about 200 pounds.

Desmond came to Kaleidoscope to get help with the transition back to his community. This occurred during a moment when I had a really self-serving need. You have to understand, at that time, Father Smith's Maryville Academy basketball team had beaten my Kaleidoscope team for four years straight. All our team members were really small and I badly needed a tall, strong youngster to play power forward. When I first met Desmond, I took one look at him and started to shake with anticipation. I said to myself, "If he can play basketball, I can finally beat Father Smith!"

Not being a saint, my very first question to Desmond was, "Do you like sports?" Desmond replied that he loved sports and said he was a very good athlete. I could see the trophy coming my way. It did occur to me, however, that I shouldn't make assumptions; maybe Desmond didn't like basketball and was into baseball or football instead. So, I asked him, "What are your two favorite sports?"

Desmond looked me right in the eye and replied, "Fencing and polo."

The people at the institution had taught Desmond to appreciate sports that fit nicely into their upper middle-class milieu. They never understood he might have to return to the inner city some day and that fencing and polo were not going to be very useful skills to him there. They were not realistically preparing him to live in his home community, where he would spend the next stage of his life.

This institution not only helped take away some of Desmond's inner-city living skills, they also played some part in losing another resource in his community—his family. This institution, like many others, believed that youth should not have any contact with their families for the first three to six months after they entered the facility. The institution thought this would help the children fit into the program more easily. Well, no one had explained this to Desmond's family, and because he had been taken from them and they had not heard from him, they felt they had lost him. When they eventually moved away, they neglected to tell people, including Desmond, where they had gone.

This nice, safe institution, which had been a good parent to Desmond for five years and had taken good care of him, had left him in a position where he had no family, few resources, and no understanding of his home community or how to fit into it anymore.

Lessons From Desmond on Community-Based Care

Desmond's story plays like a joke. In response to the question, "What are your two favorite sports?," the answer, "*Fencing and polo,*" is a punch line that most often makes people laugh. But the real joke is on Desmond, and it is not very funny. We take a young adolescent who has lived a difficult and often troubled life, help him get past those problems and perform at a high level, and then cut him off at the knees. Desmond's story gives us insight into some of the reasons we need to offer children care that is community-based[1], in the communities they know as home, and in which they ultimately will have to live.

How did we end up taking children away from their families and communities? The story of Little Orphan Annie gives us a hint. In this story, a poor ragamuffin is rescued from the orphanage by the rich Daddy Warbucks (he even took in the stray dog she had befriended), and they lived happily ever after. When I saw the musical *Annie*, I fell prey to this spirit. I fell in love with the little orphans and wanted to take them home. One hundred years ago, this type of thought led to the practice of "saving" wayward children by placing them in settings that people felt were better for them. Who would deny a child the chance to emerge from poverty to live in a safe and comfortable environment? During the era of the Great Depression, parents who were suffering hard times would drop their children off at orphanages with the promise that their children would have a better life.

We have moved to the point where we no longer put children in orphanages. Rather, we have developed welfare systems that support

---

[1] The term "community-based" is used rather broadly to describe a certain class of programs that are in a community, in distinction to being institutional or residential. However, this is not how we are using the term "community-based" here. We are referring only to those services which allow for full family participation and which preserve the child's cultural and ethnic ties to their home community. This is an important distinction that must be made when discussing this issue.

families in keeping their children at home. Foster care and adoption have become alternatives for those children for whom living at home is not deemed possible. We still cling to the fantasy that children would be better off if they lived in more affluent environments that harbor fewer risks to growing up, however. It was on this basis that Desmond was placed in a "really nice" place. He was offered all of the advantages of upper middle-class suburban living and education. Was this the best intervention for him? Let us explore why not.

After I saw the play *Annie*, I thought it could be used to recruit foster parents. I contacted a large national child welfare advocacy organization involved in foster care. They didn't agree with me. They told me that it doesn't happen the way it did in the play. First of all, children and adolescents in care often have major troubles and do not magically do better in more affluent settings. Secondly, there are not many Daddy Warbucks to go around and when such individuals are available, they don't always make the best parents for children who come from different backgrounds and are used to a different lifestyle.

I also learned from a family with whom I worked on and off for close to 20 years that an affluent environment is not necessarily the best one. Peter's adoptive parents were a well-to-do, childless couple who had decided to build a family by adopting older children who had spent years in foster care. They were blessed with the opportunity to adopt Peter, along with his three brothers and sisters, all of whom had been living in different foster homes. For these children, it was like winning the lottery. Suddenly, they were rich, living in a home with caring parents and all the advantages of their situation. Yet Peter had trouble fitting in. He found himself constantly running up against differences between his culture and lifestyle and that of his new parents. Peter ended up spending most of his postadoption years living in a group home after family dissension and his troubled response became too much for the family to tolerate. Ultimately, all but one of the children ended up similarly alienated from the family. Although many factors other than being "out of place" contributed to this, it was clear that the differences between the lifestyles of the families in which these children had originally been raised and that into which they were adopted played a major role in the family disruption.

When children are placed in an environment to which they are unaccustomed, they have two choices. They can repudiate their past and accept the values of their new family or institution, or fight to retain their old values. Peter and two of his siblings chose the latter of the two, and ended up not fitting in. The price he and others in similar circumstances pay for this is to give up a lifestyle that society has said is better than the one they came from, and to identify with a set of values which society has labeled as "bad." Inherent in this choice is a devaluation of self, parallel to the degree that society has devalued the family of origin. Peter does not know that his poor fit in his adoptive family was the result of a positive choice not to give up his family values. Instead, he thinks he's bad; after all, a "good" person would have been able to fit into the "good" family.

One of Peter's other siblings, Robert, found a way to fit into the new family. To do this he had to devalue his family of origin. It might be said that this is a good thing. As we develop, however, we gain our sense of identity from a number of sources, one of which is our genetic family and our family of early life. Many children adopted at a later age or living in long-term foster care, who have taken on the values of their new families, struggle with self-worth on the basis that their early underpinnings are perceived as being bad. As a result, Robert has never felt completely comfortable in his new identity.

Desmond had a variant of the same problem. He also fit into his more affluent lifestyle. He adapted so well to the suburban environment and had been there so long that he had assimilated that lifestyle. He had accepted the values of that slice of society. Having polo and fencing as his sports of choice defined the degree to which he accepted more affluent class values. But Desmond never got a chance to find out if he would be comfortable with his new identity because there was no place for him in that upper middle-class society. The joke played on Desmond was that no one had really planned for him to fit in. There was no Daddy Warbucks ready or willing to whisk him into a new upper-class life. There was no wealthy family to adopt him. The original goal was for Desmond to return home to the inner-city projects from which he had come. That goal had never changed, but neither Desmond nor the folks who worked with him at the institution really understood that.

Had the institution prepared Desmond to go home? Not in the least. In fact, he experienced the opposite. He was led to forsake all of the culture from which he had come. By accepting the principle that Desmond would be better off living outside of his community in a suburban environment, the well-intentioned individuals and their agency devalued his community and culture along with his lifestyle and values. They were blinded by the problems in Desmond's community and failed to understand its strengths and resources. They failed to seek strong families in that community who could have offered therapeutic foster care, nor did they help Desmond and his family deal with the problems that made their living together impossible at that time. They did not take advantage of the resources of the religious congregations and clergy in the community, which could have been offered positive local values for Desmond. They failed to find locally run youth intervention programs that could aid Desmond's development and identity using approaches that build on the strengths of African-American cultural values. Finally, they did not take advantage of local recreation programs that would have helped Desmond exercise his athletic skills in sports that could have helped him fit into the peer culture. (To be fair, I should point out that the choice of institution was more of a problem than the choice of sports offered at the institution. It would have been seen as culturally insensitive if the institution had suggested, since Desmond was African-American and came from the inner city, that basketball and football might have been better choices for him than fencing and polo.)

Desmond was not only moved out of his community, he was also moved away from his family. Desmond's "helpers" felt that the problems in his family were so troublesome that he would be better off disconnected from home. In thinking that way, they took a view of his family that only saw the family's problems, and as a result, they failed to tap the strengths in the family that could have been used to support Desmond and his needs. They chose not to utilize family preservation or in-home services that would have helped the work better with Desmond's problems. Rather, they sent him to a program that had a similarly negative view of families.

A negative approach to the families of children with emotional problems is, unfortunately, all too common. Often, the child welfare or mental health agency's first response to an emotionally troubled child is to remove that child from the family. Based on the same negative thinking, many residential and long-term hospital programs severely restrict a family's access to their child during the early months of their stay. If you remember, the program that Desmond was sent to felt that all children with problems would do better if they did not see their families for several months after they entered the program. This type of approach blames families for the troubles that their children have, based on the theory that negative relationships within the family are a large factor in children's problems. Therefore, this view holds, to be treated, such children must be isolated from the destructive interactions with their families. Although current residential treatment practice most often includes a family therapy focus aimed at helping families become more useful environments for their children, such interventions are still based on the mistaken premise that families of children with troubles are "broken" and need to be fixed. In addition, these programs are often located so far away from children's homes that it is difficult, if not impossible, for their parents to attend regularly, or at all.

As a result of this negative viewpoint, the family was ignored, and they responded by backing away. Karl's story does not tell us exactly what happened to Desmond's family, but we can surmise that they accepted the agency philosophy that they were a major cause of his problems and maybe even felt they were doing him a favor by disappearing. Like many parents of children with troubles, they had spent many frustrating years trying to help their son, and like many such parents, they were convinced that treatment away from home was the only way to save him. Additionally, because they were not included in the care, it is very possible that they got the message that Desmond would be better off without them. And when Desmond was discharged and needed them, they were gone and the system had done nothing to prevent that from happening.

While most families do not disappear as Desmond's did, we do know that residential treatment and other out-of-community programs usually devalue the family's role in helping its child. This is antithetical to the principles of Wraparound. Under the individualized service approach, we believe that families are the most important resource that a child has and that everything possible must be done to include the family in the care of its child. We believe that the positive culture and values of families are useful to children in their development and healing. We also believe that no one loves a child more than a parent. These tenets are true even when a child cannot live at home because things are not working well enough within his or her family for that to happen. In the chapter about Alex, we talked about the value of family and the need to use family strengths in the healing process. When children are living in or near their homes, those family strengths can be tapped. It is very difficult to do that when children are placed many miles from home, or even across town. Children and their families need to learn to work together, to understand each other's needs, and to respect each other's feelings. This can only be done when they are together—not during a monthly or even weekly out-of-town visit by the parents to a residential treatment center. The home is the best place for families and children to learn to understand and live with each other's problems and to take advantage of each other's strengths. When placed out of their communities, children like Desmond are deprived of the opportunity to incorporate the strengths of their family into their healing processes.

Desmond's loss of his family followed, at least in part, from his being sent to an out-of-community placement. The loss of his family left him without basic resources and support that most young adults have. Even children who are removed from their community and still have homes to return to are at peril, because the child's healing has taken place outside of the context of his or her family. They have not grown together. Because of the separation, they have often grown in different directions. Thus, many children have great difficulty fitting back into their families as they return to the community.

While Desmond's residential placement may well have provided a healing opportunity for him, it did not take into consideration where he came from and where he would eventually return. Rather, his healing took place within an environment that did not reflect the stresses that had led him to have trouble in the first place. He did not have to face the realities of life in his family or his community. Instead, his healing occurred in an atmosphere that had different types of stresses and problems—ones which he obviously was successful in overcoming. When he met Desmond, however, Karl worried that these skills were not going to be transferable to an inner-city environment. And, when we laugh about "fencing and polo," we agree.

Tori

By the age of 3, Tori[2] was already known to her neighbors as a troubled child. She always seemed to be dirty, and when she got angry, which was often, she would hit other children. One of these neighbors was concerned and called Protective Services, which sent some workers to check on Tori's mom. They found that she was a drug addict living in condemned housing. They came to the conclusion that she was not in a good position to take care of Tori, so they placed Tori in foster care. But Tori was a handful, and her behaviors did not get any better. As a result she was moved to another foster home, and then another and then another. By the time she was 12, she had been in seven different foster homes, and the social service people didn't know what to do with her. They had taken her to therapy, but that didn't help much. They took her to a psychiatrist, and that didn't do much good either. They put her in a hospital, where she began to do a little better, so they sent her back to foster care. What they didn't know, however, was that in two of her old foster homes she had been physically abused by folks trying to deal with her behavior, and worse, she was being sexually abused in the foster home they sent her back to. As a result, her behavior began to get worse again. She was diagnosed with bipolar disorder, which seemed to mean that people thought she was really crazy and had given up on trying to find a way to help her.

Finally, during her second hospitalization, she told her therapist there that she was being sexually abused. An investigation occurred, but the foster parents were exonerated, and everybody concluded that Tori's report was just the result of her craziness. She was returned to the foster home. She then began to cut herself with sharp objects and threaten suicide. She was hospitalized again and put on more medication. Then she ran away. When they finally found her, she was placed in a residential treatment center as far away from her home in Chicago as possible.

For Tori, this was the beginning of a long series of placements in various parts of the country. Like many young people in our system, she became an expert at manipulating institutions. Tori had learned that if you were stubborn

---

[2] As we wrote up Tori's story, it was clear that her identity would be very recognizable to some people, so we mixed in facts from two other young people served by Kaleidoscope in a way that did not change the point of the story but that allowed the real Tori her anonymity.

and aggressive enough, you could get yourself moved out of whatever placement you were in, and she was moved a lot. She also learned to avoid taking the pills prescribed for her by putting them in her cheeks and not swallowing them. She never really seemed to get much better.

As she approached the age of 18, the agency began to think that Tori would have to return to Chicago. But unlike Desmond, who had done well in his placement, Tori had very few skills for living in any community, no less the one from which she had come. She reacted to the news that she was going back to Chicago in her usual way: she tried to kill herself by swallowing some of the pills she had saved up. She ended up in the hospital, at which point, the Social Service folks who were her guardians called Kaleidoscope to see if we could serve her. Being a no-reject agency, we agreed, and a few days later she was sent to us.

Like many young people who are referred to Kaleidoscope, Tori did not have any experience living in the community or in fact any place outside of an institution. She had learned how to live in and manipulate institutions, but she was skeptical that she could make it in the community. She thought we were nuts when we suggested that our plan for her was to move her into an apartment in the community with some services wrapped around her, and she told us the first thing she would do if we did that was to kill herself.

We told her that we would work with her to make sure she felt comfortable and safe, and finally we convinced her that this was the best option for her. Before we moved her into an apartment, we asked her which neighborhood she would like to live in. She told us, and that's where we looked. We believe that if young people choose the community where they are going to live, they will choose places were they feel they fit in and feel comfortable. We think this will make their transition from institutional to independent living easier. They often choose the neighborhood in which they grew up, before they were sent away. This makes sense, because that is where their families live, and it is an environment in which people have similar values to their own.

Of course, once in her apartment, Tori immediately tested us: she cut herself with a knife the first week. At that time, we were checking on her rather frequently, found out what she had done, and brought her to the hospital to get sewn up. Both Tori and the hospital staff thought she needed to be hospitalized, and she asked, "Well, where are you going to send me now?"

We responded, "Back to your apartment! Only this time, we need to get rid of the knives for a while."

The first weeks and months in the apartment were harrowing for the staff as well as for Tori. Staff had to visit her in the middle of the night to calm her down. On numerous occasions, she would use anything sharp that she could find to make superficial cuts on herself and then call the staff to tell them what she had done. We made an arrangement with a nearby hospital so when she cut herself, she would immediately be taken to the hospital where they would tend to her wounds, including stitching her up, and then send her home along with her Kaleidoscope worker. Tori then escalated the situation—she took a serious overdose of the pills she had stored up. Of course, she called the agency first to let us know what she was up to, and we immediately dispatched people to the apartment and got her back to the emergency room.

In the emergency room, Tori said to us, "I guess this means that you will finally kick me out of the agency this time."

"No, since you have been saving up your pills, it's clear that you are not taking them regularly. What we're going to do is to get you off of these medications," we replied.

From that point on, services continued more smoothly. Tori talked warmly about having a one-on-one worker whose responsibility it was to help her learn independent-living skills. Up to that point, she had been unable even to shop, wash dishes, or ride public transportation. She knew nothing about the things most young people learn from their families about living in the community, either with a family or independently. We recognized how responsible she was becoming and on one occasion when my daughter needed a baby-sitter I suggested that she might choose to hire Tori for that purpose. My daughter, who spent a lot of time around Kaleidoscope, knew Tori and thought it would be an excellent idea. This was a new experience for Tori, and she found that she liked baby-sitting very much. So, we encouraged her to continue doing this and it became an important part of the process of integrating Tori back into the community.

As part of our services, we tried to get Tori involved in therapy, and she let us know that she was kind of sour on therapy, especially after the time her therapist had not believed her about her abuse. After a while she agreed to go to a therapist we know in her community who was able to connect with her and help her feel better about her community and how well she was doing in it.

Tori grew and grew. Unfortunately, because she had constantly changed institutions and never had consistent schooling, she was way behind most people her age in learning mathematics, reading, and other academic skills. Catching up was a struggle for her, but with the occasional help of a tutor, she successfully worked to close the gaps and we were able to get her enrolled in an alternative high-school program in the community, where she obtained her high-school diploma. Many youth are never able to fill those gaps when you take them out of a consistent, community-based environment and move them from placement to placement.

Tori was one of the most challenging young people to receive services through Kaleidoscope. She had a list of diagnoses as long as your arm and had been on all kinds of psychotropic medication. Prior to her coming to Kaleidoscope, it had been everyone's prediction that she would be institutionalized most of her life. Yet as crazy as she looked, it was merely her reacting to her crazy situation. As soon as she was placed back in her community and given help to stabilize her life and some good therapy to help her with her past, she showed the Kaleidoscope staff and everyone else around her that she could find her strengths and connections, live on her own in her community, and make life work for her—all of which she accomplished without medications. She found that she was a good dancer and that she could make money doing that. And even though we didn't always like the establishments in which she was dancing, she was able to make a living and support herself. Later, she gave up the dancing and started waiting tables. Most recently, Tori decided that she wanted to do better for herself and embarked on a career in real estate sales.

Lessons From Tori on Community-Based Services

As one reads Tori's story, it is easy to make fun of the agencies that sent her away, mocking their reasoning. Most of us can come up with all kinds of interventions that might have been used to avoid her long-term institutionalization. Yet just like with Desmond, well-meaning people found reason to send her away from her community. Unlike Desmond, however, Tori was never sent to really nice places and never adapted. (By this point in the book, I hope the reader sees Tori's lack of adaptation to the institutions to which she was sent as a strength.) From Tori's story, several major lessons emerge about community-based care. First, we will consider the role that placing children out of their communities plays in undermining their self-concepts and their relationships with their families. Next, we will explore how institutional living creates barriers to independent living. Lastly, we will look at how reintegration into their communities can be part of the healing process.

When Karl tells Tori's story, he offers another important reason for not sending children away from their communities. One of the common reasons for sending children away in the first place is that we do not like their behaviors and do not want to deal with them. As Karl often mentions, however, when these children come back to the community, "they will be bigger and stronger, and they will be mad that you sent them away." Karl and I agree that this is a compelling argument for not sending them away in the first place. An underlying issue here is that part of their anger is at themselves. Even if we send children away for the more altruistic reasons of wanting them to be in a "better" environment, they almost always decide that the real reason they have been sent away is because they are bad.

One teenager I knew drew me a picture that I will never forget. Peter's sister, Allison (one of the siblings adopted by the well-to-do family I discussed earlier in this chapter), had been removed from a family that abused and neglected her, had then lived in several foster homes, and was finally adopted. I was playing the Squiggle Game with her.[3] From my heart-shaped squiggle, she first drew a picture of an apple. Next she drew a hole in the apple and she finished with a worm hanging out of the hole. When I asked her to tell me the story about the worm and the apple, she told me, "the worm went to live in the apple, ate it all up inside and made it all bad, and then had to go live in another apple and made that bad, and then another and another." That was how she saw her life. Even though she had not been a troubled child and had been moved to "better" and "better" places, she still saw herself as bad and believed that this was the reason that she could not find a stable home. This feeling is common among children placed out of their homes and is a major negative consequence of traditional foster care and residential placements. Similarly, residential placements, no matter how nice, tend to be seen by children as punishment for their bad behavior.

This is also the way Tori viewed her life. Like most other neglected and abused children, Tori already felt she was being treated poorly because she was bad. When she was finally removed from the abusive

---

[3]   This is a paper-and-pencil game, devised by the child psychoanalyst D.W. Winnecott, in which the interviewer draws an undefined squiggle with a pencil. The child then turns the squiggle into a picture about which they tell a story. The roles are then reversed, and the child draws a squiggle for the interviewer to complete and tell a story about.

situation, it was her impression that she was moved not because the abuse needed to stop, but because she had done something bad. The well-meaning motivation to give her a better life had backfired. Rather than making her feel better, her placements had helped to undermine her self-esteem. Would it not have made more sense to help Tori's earlier, nonabusive foster parents learn to deal with her in a way in which she might have gotten a more positive image of herself?

Another argument for community-based approaches follows from the understanding that people feel more comfortable in environments that are familiar to them. Young people who grew up on the South Side of Chicago prefer to live on the South Side. Each neighborhood has its own character, which becomes an integral part of those who live and grow there. For most of us, when we go back to our old neighborhood, it feels good. It takes a number of years before we get that same feeling in a new place. For children who are experiencing troubles making it in life, placing them in communities that are foreign to them does not make sense. It can do nothing but make them less comfortable and give them an extra source of tension to overcome. In many instances, children are moved from one place to another in rapid succession, each time in a new community. No wonder they often have trouble settling down.

Would it not be better to look beyond the present when we make placements for children, and plan early for where the child will be when the placement ends? With Tori, that is just what Kaleidoscope did. A staff member asked Tori, "Where would you like to live?" and the final decision flowed from that discussion. Kaleidoscope's independent-living environment arranged for her to have an apartment in a neighborhood in which she felt she had roots. As a result, she felt more comfortable living there—she fit in! Any type of new placement is difficult for a child, adolescent, or young adult. Yet we can mitigate the difficulty of living in a new place, a new home, by at least making that home one in which the child will fit with the least amount of adaptation necessary.

The final lesson about community-based care that comes from Tori's story is the healing effect that reintegration into the community can have after years of institutional placement. In the story, Karl tells us that Tori's first reaction to Kaleidoscope's plan to place her in independent living was to think they were crazy. She had not developed any skills for living outside of an institution, and she knew it. As Karl says, "she had been unable to shop, to wash dishes, or to ride public transportation." We have already learned that a major problem related to placing children and adolescents in institutions for long periods of time is the failure to teach them practical skills for living in a community. Given that many youth in our systems are burdened with this handicap, the process of learning how to live in a community can lead to personal growth. Traditionally, learning independent living skills means tasks like training on how to budget one's income and balance one's checkbook. At Kaleidoscope, independent living had a broader interpretation: although Tori worked with her one-on-one helpers to improve her living skills, including those that are traditionally part of independent-living programs, she also learned how to relate to other young adults (her helpers), be a member of the community by doing things like baby-sitting, and to explore her own likes and dislikes (like dancing).

Once young people are old enough to move back into their communities and prepare for independent living, the Kaleidoscope process for helping them do this is focused on the full range of Wraparound principles. Through this experience, the youth learn their own abilities and desires, an understanding of their cultural and family backgrounds, a sense of where they fit into their communities and families, and the personal power that goes along with making their own decisions—all of which lead to a growth in their self-esteem and sense of who they are. Although it is a shame that our system's reliance on institutionalization plays a part in putting youth in the situation of needing this ego boost, it is also a wonder how a well-structured, Wraparound approach to independent living can go so far in undoing the damage.

Holding to the community-based philosophy was often a major test of Kaleidoscope's commitment to unconditional care. When Tori cut herself, she expected Kaleidoscope to kick her out like everybody else had done before. Their response was to find ways to use her community to support her better. They did this first by arranging for the hospital to be ready to sew her up when she cut herself, and later they got her off medications when she tried to overdose. In the end, the cure had nothing to do with cuttings or overdosing, it had to do with Tori learning that she was worth people sticking with her through good and bad: unconditional care.

The principles of Wraparound tell us that it would have been better if both Desmond and Tori had been able to heal in their own communities. There they could have honed their interests toward activities that would help them fit in. Additionally, they could have received help from individuals who appreciated their backgrounds rather than asking them to give those up. By living in their own communities, youth increase their skills to survive there. And most importantly, their community is a place where they can once again gain the benefits of being with or near their families.

Fully accepting a community-based philosophy is not as easy as it might appear. One major obstacle to doing so is the fact that we as a society would rather not see the troubling behaviors that most accompany young people's problems. It is easier to send these youngsters away than it is to live with the results of their behaviors in our communities. When Tori acted up in her distant placements, no one in the community saw it happen or had to deal with it. When children and youth with troubles are brought back to or kept in the community, we have to live with these disturbances, which are not always pretty. Are we ready to do this? Not always! Karl's stories often refer to his efforts to convince people in communities (sometimes child welfare case workers, sometimes police and fire departments) that it is worth keeping an individual child in the community regardless of what they might have done to make people think otherwise. Even someone as persuasive as Karl often finds this to be a very difficult sales job.

In addition to not always wanting to live with these behaviors, helping professionals are often unwilling to live with the liability risks that accompany them. Would you be willing to live with the risk of one of Tori's suicide attempts succeeding? Karl was, but the only way he could do so was to have staff on whom he could rely to make it work and obtain the other resources in the community necessary to implement a workable Wraparound plan.

The lack of resources is the third major obstacle to making a full commitment to community-based care. Part of this is purely financial. Many communities do not have enough money to spend on intensive community-based services for all the children and youth who need them to get them. The first reason for this is that not enough money is committed to child and adolescent services, period. More importantly, of the funding that is committed to services for children and adolescents, a large portion is allocated to residential treatment centers and hospitals, and little is left over to invest in community-based programs. Even when communities want to shift youngsters from institutional to community care, programs like Kaleidoscope are not there, and no money is available to start them. The issue of resources will be discussed in greater detail in a later chapter. Here, it will be sufficient to say that although Desmond and Tori ultimately readjusted to the communities where they were to live as adults (and we saw that both those adjustments had some healing qualities), both young people would have been more appropriately served if their families had been supported in taking care of them and if the youth themselves had been offered personal supports they needed to overcome their problems in their communities.

thomas, robert, and karl's friends and relatives

Stories About Cultural Competence and the Celebration of Cultural Diversity

Thomas

This story was told to me by Terry Cross, an individual for whom I have the greatest respect, as he is one of the most knowledgeable individuals about issues of cultural competence in the country and is the best trainer of those concepts I know. Terry is also a a member of the Seneca tribe from New York State who now lives in Portland, Oregon.

The story is about Thomas, a young American Indian boy whose family moved from a reservation into the city when he was about 7 or 8 years old. His family enrolled him in school in their new community. His teacher knew he had just come off the reservation and accepted him readily. She went out of her way to help him, and in recognition of his reservation-based cultural background as she understood it, she even gave him a special seat by the window because she thought he would be comforted by looking out. By the end of the first day, some of the students were complaining to the teacher that things were missing, like paper, pencils, and books. Every day more things were missing. This was unusual for this school, and the teacher became concerned. She looked everywhere for the missing items and finally discovered some of them in Thomas' desk.

The teacher asked him, "Did you steal these things?"

Thomas didn't know how to react. He became very quiet and just stood there. Finally he responded softly, "No, I didn't."

The teacher wisely decided not to do anything about it and let it pass. Things continued to disappear, however, and the teacher continued to find them at Thomas' desk. At the same time, Thomas was looking more and more depressed. At her wits' end, the teacher called in the school psychologist for help in dealing with Thomas. The psychologist talked to Thomas and agreed he appeared very depressed. She recommended he be sent to a residential treatment program.

A wise person at the school decided, before they proceeded to send him away, Thomas should talk to a man he knew, Terry Cross, who worked nearby at the Northwest Indian Institute. Terry was called and he listened to what the folks at the school had to say. He then asked if they would put Thomas on the phone.

Terry asked Thomas what was going on and Thomas told him how the missing things ended up at his desk, which did not surprise Terry. Then Terry told Thomas, "There is something you need to understand. Westerners are not like Indians. They are stingy! They think that they own everything around them."

"Is that why I keep getting into trouble?," Thomas replied.

"Yes, I think so," said Terry.

Thomas followed up by saying, "I think I understand. I can do something about that." And he did.

It turns out, in spite of their concern about Thomas' integration into city culture after growing up on the reservation, the well-meaning teacher and the others at the school didn't really understand Thomas' cultural background as well as they thought they did. He had lived on the reservation at the junction of two roads. There were several houses nearby and each of these families had a number of children who played together at the various houses. As the children played, they would often pick up toys at one house and drop them at another. If it were bedtime, the children would most often just eat and go to sleep at the house where they were, rather than go "home." You see, Thomas' tribe did not believe in private ownership—their cultural understanding was that everything belonged to everyone. Thomas was getting in trouble in school because he didn't understand the culture of the school, and they didn't know his. So, he got depressed.

Lessons from Thomas

Thomas' story always makes me sad. Not only do I ache for a little boy who is injured as people misunderstand his cultural ways and who must adjust his basic ways of life in order to survive in a new community, I also feel sorry for his teacher, who thought she was doing something special for him, only to find out that she had really missed the boat in understanding his culture and his related needs. Every time I hear Thomas' story, it leads me to engage in a moment of self-reflection about cultural issues and my own sense of cultural competence.

This happened again as I started to write this chapter, when my first reaction was to feel that I'm not really qualified to teach cultural competence. After all, I am a White, middle-class guy who was living at that time in a suburban Washington, DC, neighborhood that is almost devoid of color. I had moved there so that my children could attend the best suburban schools that public money can buy. In doing so, I restricted the degree of cultural diversity my family was exposed to. I did this in spite of the fact that I grew up in a family that believed that diversity was healthy. My parents sent me to one of the few integrated schools in the DC area during the era shortly before the end of formal segregation in the public schools. I have spent many years of my life fighting societal bigotry and racism and went through my share of "White guilt," when that was in fashion.

I am proud to say that my influence had something to do with the inclusion of cultural competence within the current system-of-care concepts for children and adolescents with serious emotional disturbance and their families, in which Wraparound service approaches have blossomed. Yet I find myself occasionally laughing at jokes with racist overtones rather than being incensed as some of my friends would be—although I would never do so in a situation where I thought an individual present could be hurt or offended. After all, I am a member of a minority group myself; I am Jewish. I get a kick out of a good "Jewish joke"—unless that joke comes from a non-Jew; then I am often offended. I think to myself, "What would I have done if I had been Thomas' teacher?"

When I complain that I have racist tendencies, Karl assures me that I am not a racist. In fact, he gives me high cultural competence ratings. Then why do I feel like I am? I have come to understand that this is because as individuals we continually view the world through the eyes of the culture in which we are raised and live. To fully comprehend cultural competence, we have to start with a basic understanding that culture does not mean skin color or ethnic heritage. All people of a particular color are not alike. For example, not only do each of the approximately 600 American Indian tribes have different cultural ways, each crossroad community, such as the one that Thomas lived in, has its own special cultural values and ways. To me, cultural competence means taking people's cultural values and styles into consideration as I try to understand who they are, what their needs are, and how to help them. Even Karl needs a reminder once in a while to fully understand this, as Karl's next anecdote will demonstrate.

The Cracker Barrel

One of the keynote speeches I was called upon to give a number of years ago was in a Southern community. Before the speech I was invited to go to brunch with a group of local folks. They took me to a restaurant called the Cracker Barrel. (It was the first Cracker Barrel that I had ever seen and I've since come to really enjoy them as place to get really fine country home cooking—the kind of cooking my grandmother used to do so well.) After being seated, I noticed my local companions were all ordering large amounts of food. They ordered smoked pork chops, grits, eggs, and pancakes. When their orders arrived at the table, the plates looked like steeples. They had so much food on them I was almost sickened by watching what they were getting ready to put away. My reaction followed from the fact that I was raised in a way where one was supposed to start your day by eating a small and very economical breakfast, not a large one.

All through the meal, I kept thinking about how many different styles of eating breakfast there are. When we were through and on our way back across the street to the meeting place, it occurred to me that breakfast was a defining part of some people's cultures. I asked myself, "What would happen if I took a child who came from that particular community and placed him in one of my yuppie foster homes in Chicago where the family actually believes one strip of bacon and two eggs have enough cholesterol to kill you?" They would probably start to feed him granola, cereal, and other nice healthy things. Then, all of a sudden, he might start acting out. Like most of the youngsters we work with, he would probably be nonverbal, so we would be unable to figure out what the problem was, and we would find the need to call in the clinicians. But the real answer to the problem would simply be that he came from a family that believed in eating large breakfasts early in the morning and he was merely reacting to his fear that we were starving him to death!

This issue came up again later when I was having a conversation with a caseworker about a family she was working with. At one point she said, "I think this family is mistreating their children."

"What makes you think that?" I asked.

"Because they never eat breakfast!" was her reply.

I inquired further, and she told me, "For three generations the men of this family worked in the coal mines and they had always preferred to work the 11 P.M. to 7 A.M. shift. As a result, the family has grown up with their clock turned around so that nobody in the entire family ever ate breakfast."

I asked, "Were the children healthy?"

"Yes," she answered.

"Were there any medical problems?"

"No," she admitted. "But," she continued, "everyone needs to eat a nice, healthy breakfast before they start their day."

I tried to be gentle and giving when I finished the conversation by telling her, "In my mind that is an unfair value judgment. You appear to be generalizing in a way that doesn't take the culture of that particular family into consideration."

What People's Breakfasting Habits Can Teach Us

The Cracker Barrel story teaches a lesson about the innumerable facets of a person's life that can become part of his or her cultural identity. While skin color, religion, and ethnic heritage have become the primary aspects of culture on which we focus, almost every aspect of a person's life must be taken into consideration when understanding and helping that person deal with life's problems. This is not always so easy for each of us to do. Karl admitted that the diet of his colleagues who ate with him at the Cracker Barrel initially made him physically sick. These things happen to us because our own personal ways of doing things are ingrained lessons that we have learned from our families and other significant people in our lives. Karl's next story gives us further insight into how this comes about.

Grandma

I think it's very important that we look at the value and diversity of people, but this is not always easy. Our families do not even have to specifically tell us that something is the right or the wrong way, they simply tell us that it is our way, and as we grow up, we tend to internalize those lessons. For example, my grandmother was a wonderful and warm person who cared a lot about people. She also had the fastest and furthest reaching hands in the world. I believed that no matter where I was in the country, my grandmother had the ability to reach out and slap me for saying things that she felt were inappropriate. So, I always refrained from even suggesting the things I'm about to say until after she passed away.

In addition to all of her loving characteristics, my grandmother was also one of the most culturally incompetent people that I have known. She believed that there were only two kinds of people in this world: Methodists and other people. Now, she never directly suggested to us that there was something wrong with non-Methodists, but she had her ways of demonstrating it. For example, I got married to a Methodist girl and my brother didn't. Guess who got the better wedding present? Of course, I did. These are the kind of things our families attempt to teach us without even realizing what they are doing. In order to serve children from other families, we need to look past our own ingrained personal family values.

Lessons About Personal Style

Getting past our own ingrained personal family values is a tough task, and most of us are just like Grandma—there is our way and there is everybody else's way. And, regardless of how old we are or the degree to which we have accepted diversity, we fear the reprisals of Grandma's slap when we stray from what our family has defined as acceptable. For most of us this is not a conscious process. Unless we are openly bigoted, as some are, our biases tend to be buried under the surface, and—as in Karl's experience at the Cracker Barrel—only become exposed when we are directly faced with them. One of our responsibilities is to recognize the differences between our own personal style and that of others so that we make judgments about others only after we have figured out which differences matter and which do not.

Who is right about eating breakfast, the social worker in the Cracker Barrel story or the miner's family? Each time we come up against such a judgment, the culturally appropriate thing to do is to step back, and before making a decision, ask Karl's questions about how things are going. As a society, we have made decisions that certain very specific family ways of doing things are unacceptable and must be stopped. These are limited to physical and sexual abuse and neglect. For all other things, there are no easy answers. To make appropriate and objective decisions about these things, we first need to understand our own biases and how they affect our decisionmaking.

A family worker with whom I worked in a family preservation program told me a story. She complained that she was having a fight with a state child protection worker about a family. Apparently, the family was living in a home that had a large hole in the living room floor. The child protection worker felt that the hole was dangerous and wanted the family to move (an impossible task at the time), or she would remove the children. The family preservation worker was not as concerned. She saw this as a good, strong family that had come across bad times and was stuck, at least for the short term, in a home with deficiencies. The children all knew about the hole and its dangers and took care not to fall into it. They had lived with the hole for a long time without it causing much trouble; it was just a fact of life for the family. Who would you side with, the family preservation or the child protective worker? The correct answer is not obvious, but the dilemma is very common.[1]

Cultural competence is essential to the delivery of any service to a child and his or her family. This is a high standard to reach, given that cultural competence is an endpoint of a continuum of cultural approaches that range from Cultural Incapacity on one end to Advanced Cultural Competence, or Cultural Proficiency, on the other end. In between, there are all degrees of cultural competence, each of which presents its own inherent dangers. The next few stories will illustrate the various degrees and their potential pitfalls.

Robert

One of the young people we served at Kaleidoscope was Robert, an African American youth in our independent-living environment. At one point in time, Robert wanted his Department of Social Services caseworker to do a certain thing for him. No matter what Robert tried, the worker wouldn't do it. Robert had even attempted to get the caseworker's supervisor to do it, but to no avail. When Robert told me this story, my first response was to offer to negotiate for him at Social Services.

[1] I believe that in the end, the family preservation worker convinced the child protection worker that the family had many strengths and that protection of the children from the hole in the floor was not a major issue and the family was allowed to stay in their home. In Wraparound, money would have been found or someone would have volunteered to fix the hole—I don't remember if that happened in this case.

He said, "No, Karl, don't worry about it. Anyway, it wouldn't do any good."

Now I know a lot of people at Social Services, some of whom will do me a favor now and then and others who respond to my influence, so I thought that I could have helped Robert. But, I was interested in why he didn't think I could help—maybe he knew something about his particular situation that I didn't—so I replied, "Why don't you think it will help?"

"Well, you know, Karl, both my worker and her supervisor are White."

"So what?," I asked.

Robert kind of gave me a 'Duh' look and answered, "We're both Black!"

Robert had become convinced that Black people had no power in a White world. It was his perception that any power that I might have as the Executive Director of a major agency in the city would be automatically negated by the fact I was Black. Robert had truly become a victim of the racism under which he had lived all of his life.

Degrees of Cultural Competence

Cultural Incapacity basically describes a state in which one's approach to others is ruled by personal biases—in other words, racism. The dangers on this end of the continuum are obvious to anyone with the slightest degree of cultural competence. Imagine a Ku Klux Klan member imposing his or her own personal biases on an African American child and family, a neo-Nazi on a Jewish child, or a Northern Irish Protestant on a Catholic child. As a society, minority group members are already victims of the racism around them, a condition that often has a deleterious effect on their mental health. If we then add racism in a "helping" setting, one of two things is bound to follow: either the help will not be accepted, or worse, the "help" will compound the original damage from the societal racism. Karl's story about Robert illustrates how Cultural Incapacity in our society has left its mark on our children.

The next step up on the cultural competence continuum is Cultural Blindness. This state is a more hopeful, but still dangerous. At this level, helping people put their biases behind them, and instead have accepted the premise that cultural differences are unimportant—we are all alike! Are we? Of course not. Not only does this blind condition deny any strengths that emanate from differences, but it also has the danger of making any difference seem pathological in nature, like everybody having to have the same kind of breakfast. While it is nice to view us as equal members of one unified society, we are all made stronger by our differences, many of which add significantly to society. The social worker who worried about the miner's children eating breakfast in the Cracker Barrel story suffered from a form of Cultural Blindness.

Another stage along the Cultural Competence continuum is Cultural Precompetence. Here the differences in culture are understood and appreciated, yet not well applied. Thomas' teacher was an example of this type of cultural problem. She made the assumption that because Thomas was American Indian, he would have specific needs and like specific things. She understood that because Thomas was American Indian and came from a reservation he might have trouble adapting to a non-Native, urban setting, and this is laudable. She blew it, however, when she made assumptions based on her preconceived notions of what Thomas' needs as an American Indian were, when in reality she had no understanding at all of the culture of his particular tribe and community and the aspects of it that could (and did) cause him trouble in his new setting. As soon as a more culturally competent approach was applied to Thomas and his situation, things began to make sense to him and ultimately worked out better for him.

Even at this middle level of cultural competence, people fall prey to their own stereotypes of various cultural groups. Karl reminds people when he teaches about cultural competence, "There are many different Indian tribes in the country and they are not all the same. They have different values and customs. Similarly, there are many different Spanish-speaking groups, and the fact that their language is the same does not mean that their customs are the same. Stereotypes are very dangerous."

Near the top end of the continuum of cultural competence is Basic Cultural Competence. When someone reaches this level, they recognize and accept the differences among individuals from different cultures. In addition, they recognize the need to address each individual's culture individually and to have an understanding that cultural values and practices are not uniform among all peoples from a particular cultural group. Then it gets more complicated. For once we learn about a particular culture, we need to remember that cultural values and practices change over time and our knowledge needs to be continually updated or relearned.

To be truly culturally competent, to have reached the stage of Advanced Cultural Competence or Cultural Proficiency, one must recognize individuals' differences as strengths and accept the premise that culture makes a family strong, even if it is a markedly different culture than yours. Karl's next story illustrates part of this principle.

Karl's Friends

Probably the most startling lesson for me about cultural competence occurred some years ago at a time when Ira directed the National Institute of Mental Health's Child and Adolescent Service System Program, or CASSP, as it was commonly known, and which is described in better detail in Chapter 10. This program's purpose was to create a better way for states and communities to meet the needs of the most troubled children and their families. One of the program's goals was to ensure that the services provided to these folks would be culturally appropriate. CASSP funded a technical assistance center at the Georgetown University Child Development Center, which brought together a committee of people of color to figure out how to fulfill this particular goal. This group decided the best approach would be to focus on the new concept of cultural competence. Ira challenged the group to define what they meant by cultural competence. The committee responded by deciding to write a monograph on the topic.

Four people from the group were picked to write the monograph, three African-Americans and one American Indian. They were Mareasa Isaacs, who was at that time the child mental health director for the State of New York; Barbara Bazron, who then was the director of a special education demonstration in Pittsburgh called PACE; myself; and Terry Cross, who was working at the Northwest Indian Institute in Portland, Oregon, and who was the group's appointed leader. We discovered we were all going to be attending the same conference, and we planned to come in a day early to outline the monograph and assign writing tasks that would allow us to then go our separate ways to finish our assigned work.

So we cloistered ourselves, turned off the phone, and started to work. We progressed well throughout the day, and by the end I thought we had really accomplished a tremendous amount of work. As we were finishing up, the three African-Americans realized that Terry had hardly said a word all day, and one of us asked, "Terry, is anything wrong? Don't you like what we've done?"

He thought for a few moments and then turned to us and said, "This has been a wonderful day and I feel good about what we have accomplished, but you need to know I sometimes have trouble working with Black people."

We didn't understand what the problem was and asked him to explain it to us.

Terry said, "In Seneca Indian culture, people tend to wait at least five seconds after someone stops talking before the next person starts. This is very important, because this is how you demonstrate you have heard what they have said and that you've really thought about it." He continued, "When I work with Black people, as soon as one person stops talking another one starts, and if I hold to my own cultural values, I never get a chance to say anything."

We all agreed it was important for us to honor Terry's cultural value by trying to remember to wait the proper time so he could participate fully. It was not easy, and we all ended up laughing about it.

About a month later, I happened to be with my colleague and friend, Beth Stroul. I was telling this story to Beth, and about the time I was halfway through the story, she started to laugh and I asked her why.

"Karl," she replied, "you need to understand that with Indians, it's five seconds; with Blacks, it's as soon as someone else finishes; but we Jews, we tend to interrupt."

We laughed and I just kind of filed it away in the back of my mind. A couple of months later I happened to be out in California and I was talking to another friend and colleague, Mario Hernandez, who, incidentally, had been part of the cultural competence committee that had sponsored the monograph. I was discussing cultural competence with him and told him the story about Terry and Beth.

I got to the point where I was saying, "...culturally, we need to understand that in some instances, Indians need five seconds, Blacks tend to talk right away, and Jews tend to interrupt," when Mario began to laugh.

"Well Karl, you need to understand that with Indians it's five seconds, with Blacks it's right away, and Jews may interrupt, but we Cubans, we all talk at the same time."

These experiences started me thinking about what would happen if I, as an African American, were a school teacher and I had four students: an African American, an American Indian, one of Jewish descent, and a Cuban American. When I asked a question, the American Indian might wait five seconds before answering the question because that was part of his value system, and as a result, he may never get the chance to let me know he had the answer. In addition, as an African American, my assumption would be that most people would answer the question right away if they knew the answer, so I would assume he did not know the answer. The African American child would answer the question right away. This would make sense to me. The Jewish child might have interrupted me in the middle of asking the question, maybe even blurting out the right answer. I would have considered it rude, become irritated with that child, and not listened to or given credit for the answer. The fourth child, the Cuban American, might have been talking the whole time I was talking and may have even answered the question by the time I had finished asking it. However, I would assume it was time to call in the clinicians and get this child on some medication. In reality, all four of these children would know the answer, but I would have responded to each of them differently, based on my own cultural biases. This is to suggest that when people respond differently than we do, we should explore their cultural values and customs, value their diversity, and respond to them accordingly.

After one of my presentations, a woman walked up to me smiling. She proceeded to say that there was some other group that I needed to know about. She said, "It may be very true about Indians five seconds, Blacks right away, Jews interrupting, and Cubans at the same time. But I'm English, and in England people would not have said anything until after you had left, and then they would have proceeded to talk about you." I just keep finding new little gems to add to this story.

Celebrating Diversity

When Karl tells this delightful story, he is quick to follow-up with the warning from earlier in this chapter, "Stereotypes are dangerous!" He reminds us that all American Indians, African Americans, Jews, and Cuban Americans are not the same, and just because someone fits into one of these particular categories does not mean that he or she will act the same way as told in the story.

As Karl comes to the end of the story, he leaves us with two other lessons. The first of these repeats the warnings from earlier in this chapter—if we are not careful, our own cultural underpinnings, experiences, and biases may unfairly influence the way we perceive people from backgrounds different than our own. The second lesson is a positive one—after we explore peoples cultural values and customs, *we should value their diversity*. It is this second lesson that defines the highest level of cultural competence: Advanced Cultural Competence or Cultural Proficiency.

Everyone enjoys the spirit of this story and can construct an addition to it based on his or her own personal cultural experience. When we respond to the story with laughter, we join with Karl in celebration of cultural diversity. How wonderful it is that each of us is different and how much more sense it makes to enjoy those differences rather than denying or fighting them. In life we have a choice. We can hate people who are different from us, we can deny the fact that they are indeed different, or we can appreciate their differences and learn from them. For the most part, our society has a tendency to assimilate differences and to become more homogeneous—for example, even the most racist among us ends up incorporating into their language words from Ebonics, the dialect of inner-city African Americans, or from Yiddish, the ancestral language of Eastern European Jews.

In Wraparound, cultural competence at the highest levels is essential. When we are Culturally Proficient, our celebration of diversity allows us both to take advantage of the resources that individual's culture offers them and permits us to truly individualize our approach to all individuals and families who require assistance. In both earlier and later chapters, we present the concept that for Wraparound to be effective and efficient (cost effective), we must take advantage of every resource that each individual, family, and community has. Cultural values and practices of families and communities fall high upon the list. Whether these values are based on religious beliefs and/or affiliations or have to do with a community set of nonreligious values, they need to be incorporated into the set of resources that can be brought to bear. A religious belief can offer a great deal of strength and/or comfort under trying circumstances. If we do not know about the power of those beliefs or the degree to which a particular individual accepts and uses them, we are at a loss to help that individual reach his or her potential. The same is true for ethnically determined values and coping mechanisms. First, we have to recognize them and then we have to see how individuals choose to use them in their personal lives. If we do not take advantage of the strengths in people's differences, we lose that important part of their available resources.

Karl's stories elucidate the full range of cultural competence issues and reminds us that we need to be aware of and concerned about all of them. On one end, these include the dangers of cultural insensitivity, whether it is a result of cultural blindness or out-and-out racism. On the other end, they include waste inherent in the failure to be culturally proficient enough to take advantages of the strengths embedded in every cultural grouping. Imagine the boost to Thomas' self-esteem if his new school had not only recognized and adapted for his cultural value of sharing, but if it had also used this value to teach all of the children in his class the values of sharing and their benefits to both the American Indian culture as well as other cultures! Then imagine the benefit to the culture at large.

andrew and george

Stories About Meeting Clients' Needs Through
Child and Family Teams

Andrew

Wraparound is not a process that somebody thought up one day; rather, it
has evolved over a period of time. One of the elements of Wraparound that
emerged late was the Child and Family Team. When Wraparound first began
as a formal process, communities usually had one single interagency
coordination team, which acted as a gatekeeper for getting the most intensive
services and did most of the intervention planning. All families who wanted
high-intensity services for their children, including the newly emerging
Wraparound services, had to have their requests submitted to this team, which
would then create a plan for them.

One of the things we realized about these community teams was that
the material about families that was submitted to them for review almost
always presented only the problems and what was wrong with the child. The
team never got to hear about the child's strengths and what was going right
for him or her. At Kaleidoscope, we realized that the people who had contact
with the child or family—the people who knew their strengths and could
therefore be of most help to them—were not present at the team meeting. It
might be the schoolteacher who served the child last year, it might be the
therapist who had been working with a child for a number of years, it might
be the neighbor next door, it might be a grandparent, or it might be someone
else who we wouldn't even have thought of. If we were going to balance the
services and base them on strengths, we needed to know the positive
information these individuals had to offer.

To make sure that the most useful and important people for the family
were included in the care, we decided we would pull together those people

who were closest to the child and the family, and they would have the responsibility for putting the services together. We started using what is now called a Child and Family Team. Once we started to move in that direction, the other benefit we realized was that all of the services provided to a child and family did not need to be formal services. The team concept allowed us to use informal services as part of the process, and what followed was that we realized we could use the family themselves as caregivers.

One of the things I do is to travel around the country doing two- and three-day Wraparound trainings with my wife, Kathy, during which we demonstrate to people how this Child and Family Team process works. We do this by asking the training's organizers to bring in a family and child who are having problems that have proven difficult to solve. We hope to put a plan together with them, and for this process we require two things. The first is for the family to pick out the people who are going to be part of the team that will plan for them. Secondly, we ask for a commitment from the training planners to implement whatever plan the team comes up with, so we don't set up families by giving them hope and then not following through.

In one instance, just before a family was brought into the training where we were going to put a Child and Family Team together for them, we became aware that the people who planned this training had set it up so the family would sit in a little circle in the center and the people who were attending the training were to sit in a larger circle around them. More than one hundred people were going to be sitting around the edge in the larger circle—a fact about which I became very nervous.

When I was introduced to the mom, I said to her, "The way they have this set up is really going to be pretty rough and was not what I had anticipated. I apologize to you, and to tell you the truth, considering that what you are dealing with your life, if I were you, I don't think I would do it."

She smiled and asked, "You wouldn't do it?"

I said, "Yes."

She said, "In that case, I will." I saw this as a strength!

So we sat down. She had brought her two children to the meeting, as well as her boyfriend, to whom the written material referred as her "paramour" (I find this to be an outdated word with really negative connotations). As we started to talk about why we were there, it became very clear that the people who had brought the family in wanted to focus only on the problems and not on the strengths. As they saw it, the problem was that the older youth, Andrew, was extremely dangerous. As an example, they talked about how he had tied up his foster parent, left him tied on the bed, and run away. What made this worse was his foster parent was handicapped and needed to be in a wheelchair. My first thought was, "How dangerous could this youngster be if people had placed him in a foster home where the primary caretaker was wheelchair-bound?"

The gentleman in the wheelchair was at this meeting, and the first question I asked was to him. "Just how did he tie you up?" I asked.

He responded, "Andrew just lifted me up and put me on the bed. At first, he lay me on my stomach and I told him that was very dangerous for me. So he gently rolled me onto my back."

Next, I wanted to find out something about Andrew's runaway behavior. The only thing the written material said about it was simply that he had run away. When I asked about it, his mother joined the conversation, "He wasn't running away! He was really coming to protect me because the kids in school had been taunting him and told him that if he didn't do what they wanted him to do, they would hurt me, and he was terrified for me."

I asked, "How did he wind up in the system in the first place?"

"Well, he was getting in a lot of fights at school," said his mother.

I said, "Fights with kids younger or kids older?"

She said, "Only kids who were his age or older. Andrew would never touch anyone younger than him; that's how he was brought up."

"Oh, wow!" was my reaction. I followed by asking, "Does he ever hit his little brother?"

She said, "Oh no, Andrew would never touch his little brother either."

By this time, we had begun to form an opinion of this young man: 1) he was really interested in protecting his mom, 2) he did not fight with his little brother, and 3) although when he got really angry he would kick a hole in a wall or put a fist through a wall, he never attacked family members or smaller defenseless children at all. In reality, he hadn't even attacked his foster parent. It didn't make sense that this was a boy who was presented to us as needing to be sent away and institutionalized.

We then started to talk to Andrew. We wanted to find out what he really cared about. One of the things that I noticed was the fact he liked to fish and he never got to go fishing anymore. I asked, "When you did go fishing, who did you go fishing with?"

"Well, I went fishing with John." John was Mom's boyfriend. "But," Andrew explained, "I never get to do that any more."

I turned to John, who hadn't said anything the whole time we were sitting there, and asked, "John, how come you stopped taking him fishing?"

"Because they no longer let me," he replied.

It is amazing that the people working with Andrew's family would set up a situation in which a resource such as John would be written off. The only reason I can think of is that these helping people did not have a favorable opinion of him or Andrew's mother. You see, mom did not have the most feminine occupation—she was a truck driver. She drove those big trailer trucks up and down the highway, and I think in some ways this had something to do with the way people felt about her. I don't think the people in the community could view her and her "paramour" as a family or think that John's presence might be helping. Rather, John was perceived negatively and Andrew had been moved away from him and Mom—into foster care.

I asked Andrew, "What do you like about fishing?"

He said, "It calms me down, and I don't get so angry." Thus, part of the plan became for John to be allowed to pick him up two or three evenings a week and take him fishing.

I had just started to believe that putting this plan together was going to be pretty simple, when Mom made a chance comment suggesting that both of the children had been in therapy.

I asked, "The younger child, why was he in therapy?"

She said, "He was in therapy because he had started to act out himself."

"What did he do?" I followed.

"He would leave the house and run away into the woods," she replied.

Then someone mentioned that when this younger brother ran away, he would take with him all the food in the refrigerator. He was only 12 years old and had been known to eat a whole ham.

The boy's therapist was at the training and he said he had not heard about the boy gorging himself on food like that.

It became clear that we needed to start providing more appropriate services for this young man also. What was strange about this whole process was that the professionals who were sitting around the table had not communicated with each other and had not looked to see what other family members (including John) were available to provide some care for Andrew. As a result, they were in the process of sending him into an institution—a level of care that, in my opinion, he did not need.

George

Another family with whom we were privileged to sit around the table, using the same type of process, had a 12-year-old boy who had in been in a residential program that cost in the neighborhood of $160,000 a year. His records suggested that he was extremely difficult and hard to get along with. He was on more medication than any 12-year-old I had ever run across. The people from the residential institution were ready to send this boy home, but they had a major concern: they had put together a complicated behavior modification program for him and felt that his mother had not heard what they had said about it and would not be able to carry it out. So, we suggested that we pull together a Child and Family Team.

The people who sat around the table were an incredibly interesting group. We had asked Mom to bring with her those people who supported her because we feel it is important that the people to whom we are providing services have their personal support system at the table as well as their more formal professional supports. In this particular case, mother came along with a delegation of her two sisters and her minister. We also had the professionals around the table—we had someone from the school, a therapist, a child welfare worker who had worked with the family, and a couple of people from the residential program—and, so we were now ready to work.

As we began, in came a young man who was so drugged up that he simply walked across the room, climbed up into my wife Kathy's lap and went to sleep. As we sat down, we had everyone introduce themselves, which is the first thing we always do. Next, I gave a summary of how we work.

When I was finished, it was time to start, and I said to mother, "The first thing I like to do is list the strengths of every member of the family on the wall; is it okay for us to get started?" And she indicated, yes.

As I rose to begin the task of putting the family strengths up on the wall, one of the mother's sisters said, "No, you can't get started yet."

I asked, "Why?"

She said, "Well, you need to understand that I'm in charge."

And I said, "Okay."

She said, "Our mother is in charge of everyone in this family, and since she is at home taking care of the other children today, she told me that I was to be in charge at this meeting."

And I said, "Yes, ma'am. Well, is it okay now if I put the strengths up on the wall?"

And she said, "No. What I want to talk about first is that we want George off of the medication. He seems to be doped up a lot and we don't think this medication is good for him."

I looked at George sleeping on Kathy's lap and asked, "Does he need all of this medication?"

In response to my question the people from the residential program became very alarmed, and one of them said, "Well, you don't seem to understand, he really needs the medication. He can't get along without it. If he doesn't get it, we have had tremendous problems keeping him under control, and he is often a danger to others and to himself when he is out of control." They had already expressed their concerns about Mom not having the skills to implement the wonderful behavior management program they had put together. They went on to explain again that it was going to be extremely difficult for George to make it if he was not on medication, that he really needed the medication, and it was important for him to continue taking it.

In response, the aunt gave a grunt and said with some contempt, "Well, you need to know, when you sent him home at Christmas and at other holidays and in the summertime, the first thing we did was take him off the medication."

It got extremely quiet in the room. I looked at George's aunt and asked her, "Well, they suggested he really needs the medication, but you're suggesting that you take him off of it. When you don't give him the medication, does he ever go off?"

She answered, "Sure, he goes off."

I followed, "Isn't that a problem?"

She retorted, "Of course that's a problem, but that's why my other sister is here with us today. Because she's really good with the boys in the family, and when he goes off, she comes over and sits with him and works with him until she gets him calmed down."

And I said, "That's great, I guess she lives real close."

She said, "Oh no! In fact, she lives on the other side of town from George, with me and my mom."

I said, "Well, how long does it take her to get over to George when he goes off?"

"About an hour—if traffic is good," she answered.

Now, at this point I am thinking about crisis intervention time, and I know that anytime it takes longer than 45 minutes to intervene in a crisis, I get skeptical about whether or not you are really providing crisis intervention. So, I said, "Well, that's really too bad."

The aunt replied off-handedly, "Yeah, it would be better if we lived closer. You know, my mom always wanted us to live together so George and his mother could be in the house as well. We had talked at one point about building out the basement, but unfortunately we didn't have the money."

It was at that moment the minister raised his head and said, "Wait a minute. Let me see if I understand this. The problem here is that you need to build out the basement and make an apartment there?"

We said, "Yes."

He continued, "Well, I've got a guy in my congregation who owns a lumber yard, and I'm sure he would donate the building materials it would take to get the job done. Also, I've got all these retired plumbers, electricians, and carpenters who are always looking for something to do. I bet that if we asked them, we could get them to build out your mom's basement and then George and his mother could move in with the rest of the family."

And actually, that is what happened. We heard months later that the basement had been built into an apartment into which the child and the mother moved. George was close to his family, and he was off a lot of the psychotropic medication he had been on. A child who had been costing the state $160,000 per year was now only costing somewhere in the neighborhood of $17,000 or $18,000 a year. But the key to this process was that Mom had brought her informal supports to the process: her two sisters and her minister.

Lessons on the Value of Child and Family Teams

I had always wondered why, when Karl talks about Child and Family Teams, he almost always chooses to tell about experiences that happened during training demonstrations on the road, rather than talk about the Child and Family Teams that he used in the Kaleidoscope program. Then as I was working on these two stories for this book, it struck me how easy it appeared for Karl to discover solutions for the most difficult situations that people present to him in these demonstrations. Indeed, I am always awestruck when I hear these stories, and I assume that Karl chooses to tell these particular stories because he is similarly impressed with the simplicity with which "thrown-together" Child and Family Teams can come up with solutions for complex problems. Of course, the first reaction of most people who hear these stories is to give Karl the credit for having amazing insight and the ability to formulate the most relevant questions, and he certainly deserves it; that is not at all what the stories are about, however. Rather, the real insight that Karl brings has less to do with the content of what is in the stories than with the fact that he had the foresight to bring all those people, including the families, to the table. They are the ones who really make the solutions easy.

These stories point out that the solutions to the problems become easy when you have the right tools to work with. How many times have you said while trying to fix something that has gone wrong or construct something new in your home, "If I only had the right tool!" Or, the opposite, when the right tool is there to complete a complicated job, "Boy, having the right tool sure made that easy!" How difficult would it be to nail two boards together if the only tool you had was a screwdriver? Sure, you could work on the problem, and if you were extremely lucky, you might even be able to use the screwdriver like a hammer and get the nails far enough in to hold the boards together to some degree. You might even figure out that it might be better to screw the boards rather than nail them—of course, that can only work if you can find the right screw. In human services, the budgetary limitations that are placed on public agencies most often keep us from having the right tools to do the job. Often, we ignore the right tools when we have them and continually try to nail the two boards together with a series of wrong tools, a screwdriver this time, a saw the next time, and maybe even a crowbar—a tool usually used for wrecking. As a result, the boards never get put together securely. The Child and Family Team is the most important mechanism for making sure you have the right tools when trying to help children and their families find solutions to their complicated problems.

The wonder in these two stories is that Karl tells us that the tools were there all along, and we never used them. Both stories demonstrate that the correct tools were dismissed as being bad and had been rejected. John was not seen as a corrective agent for Andrew; he was seen merely as a "paramour" and thrown away. George's aunts were never recognized as the best tool for crisis stabilization; instead, they were seen as impediments to use of an inadequate tool—overmedication. Only by bringing all of the people involved with the family together could the proper tools ever be discovered or used.

The Child and Family Team is a mechanism for ensuring that the basic tenets of Wraparound can be practiced. They allow for unconditional care. The team ensures this by including those individuals who have always been there for the child and family—those who have demonstrated that they will not give up on them. For a child, the most unconditional care comes from their parents and other family members. The team is *not* called the "Child and Professional/Community Agency Team" for a good reason. We cannot rely on nonfamily members to have the commitment to stick with children to the same degree that families can and will. Family members do not go home at five o'clock. Those family friends and community professionals who have demonstrated over time their unconditional commitment to the child and family also make good Child and Family Team Members.

Family focus and family strengths are a major purpose of the Child and Family Team. The unconditional nature of family bonds has been discussed earlier in this book. In addition, families have strengths that they bring to the team. John (whom *we* see as a family member, unlike the community professionals where he lived) has a positive relationship with Andrew that can and should be used in solving problems. The aunts in George's story have the knowledge and capacity to deescalate him, and the solution to his problems includes facilitating their participation in his care.

Using Child and Family Teams encourages a strength-based approach toward the child. This occurs because the team is comprised of those family members, community friends, acquaintances, and professionals who have recognized those strengths in the past. By including these positive individuals, the team will not be allowed to forget the family's strengths. Of course, some individuals on the team may not be so optimistic. For example, a child's current probation officer, child welfare case worker, therapist, or teacher all need to be on the team but may choose to focus more on the problems and negative issues. It's important to remeber and plan for the other, problematic, side of reality; however, the positive influence of the team will put the negatives in a perspective that recognizes and focuses heavily on the child's strengths. In the first story, Andrew did tie up his foster parent. While there is a problematic side to this action, some team members will ensure that no one forgets or casts aside the strength-based side of his concern for the man's physical needs. And although some may be concerned about the boy running away, others will be there to give him positive credit for doing it to protect his mother.

The members of a well-constructed Child and Family Team will ensure that the interventions will be truly individualized. This occurs because the team is not wholly made up of professionals or representatives of programs, who often bring with them a singular point of view that leads to very few options for intervention. The team also includes a group of nonprofessionals who bring with them capacities and approaches that come out of their own backgrounds and are based on their ongoing relationship with the child. They also bring with them many refreshing new options for intervention. George's aunt had never heard the term "deescalation," nor did she know about the professional tools of behavior modification and medication. Her tool was her relationship with the child and her ability to "be really good with the boys of the family." Whatever "being really good with the boys" means, it is certainly an intervention that can work to meet this boy's unique needs and be enhanced by moving them closer together.

Cultural competence is a very difficult balance to reach because each individual and family has its own unique culture. The inclusion of the individuals from the family and community who represent the child's culture on the Child and Family Team assures that the plan that is created is not only respectful of their culture but also takes advantage of cultural resources that are available to them. The culture of Andrew's family produced a value about not hurting younger children that became identified as one of the boy's strengths. The power of that particular value within that family's culture needed to be recognized and respected in order to use it in planning ways to meet the child and family's needs.

The Child and Family Team is by nature community-based. Both stories demonstrate how reliance on family members and other community-based individuals can have a major impact in making it possible for a child with troublesome behavior to live in the community, and in these cases with his family. The team's importance in allowing this to happen goes beyond the inclusion of family and professionals who are positively oriented toward the child and family. What truly allows the team to construct community-based interventions is the inclusion of those individuals from the community who have the mandate to protect the child and the community (such as child welfare and juvenile probation workers). While these individuals may not always see the family or child in a positive light (especially at the beginning of Wraparound intervention), they serve an important role on the team in reminding it of the issues that need to be addressed for the child to live in the community and/or with his or her family. These issues most often are in the area of safety, and it becomes an important task for the team to come up with strategies for meeting the personal safety needs of the child and other family members and the general safety of the community. When the individuals who are mandated by law to protect the child and the community are included as team members, the community as a whole, and as represented by public child protective and juvenile justice agencies, can feel comfortable about the community-based nature of the intervention plan.

The use of community resources can act to make the care extremely cost-efficient, a basic premise of Wraparound, and the Child and Family Team enhances their use. While cost-efficiency alone is not a reason in itself for having a Child and Family Team, the team's structure is inclusive of individuals from the community who have access to a wide range of free or low-cost resources. The best example of this was the inclusion of the minister in the team planning for George. When the team recognized that the major impediment using George's aunt for crisis stabilization was the existence of a basement apartment for George and his mother in the aunt's house, the minister knew the resources that could be called upon to make it happen. Without these free resources, the problem would never have been solved so easily; no community agency would be free to use its resources to add on to someone's house. But the Child and Family Team allowed these tools to be at the table in the first place and used in the second place. These cost-efficient solutions to problems are vital to making the flexible and individualized planning that goes with Wraparound feasible. If one relied solely on public funds for the implementation of intervention plans, many of their most exciting and potent aspects could never happen.

Constructing and Running the Child and Family Team

The practice of constructing and running a Child and Family Team is an important aspect of Wraparound. Karl and his wife, Kathy, do a training about the construction and use of these teams based on principles that have become common practice in Wraparound. To give the reader an idea of the elements, structure, and process of forming and running a Child and Family Team, the outline of this training follows.

What Makes Child and Family Teams Work?

Four characteristics of the Wraparound process make Child and Family Teams work: Access, Ownership, Voice, and Consistency. All of these are geared toward the child and the family being a vital part of the process. The lessons about family focus that we learned from Alex's and Shirley's story earlier in this book all come to life on the Child and Family Team. Through *access*, the team ensures that the parent and child both have a valid option of inclusion in the decisionmaking process. As I understand it, this means that the plan will not work unless the family members feel that they are an important part of the intervention planning process. This ultimately leads to *ownership*. Through the family's participation, the team ensures that the parent and child will agree with and are committed to any plan that concerns them. For this to happen, the family must have *voice*, which allows the parent and child to feel that they are heard and listened to at all junctures of planning. Finally, the process must be one in which the parent and child are served by a *consistent* team of workers for the services and crisis.

Karl and Kathy emphasize in their trainings that the Child and Family Team must be more than just a name for a process; rather, the team must represent a group of people who are working together toward a joint mission, and the family, the parent(s) and child, must be true members of that team. When all of these elements come together for a family, the Child and Family Team gains the power to make interventions that will truly build on the strengths of children and their families and will lead to interventions that they can use to better meet their needs.

Working with Families

Nonfamily team members often have trouble understanding how to work with families, even when they understand how important it is and they have the desire to do so. Most of us were trained within the concepts of a deficit model, which at best is neutral toward the role of children and their families. To help us all learn how to be inclusive, Karl and Kathy suggest the following strategies for working with families. A parent named Creasa Reed actually gave Karl and Kathy the first version of this list of "do's and don'ts," and other parents have since added to it.

- Take the time to form opinions about a family
- Be direct
- Trust the family's instincts
- Speak language that families understand
- View families in the context of their whole life, rather than as "cases"
- Assist families to develop "life plans," not "treatment plans"
- Support the family's ownership of their plan
- Identify and reinforce the family's strengths
- Involve families in every level of planning
- Keep families informed
- Celebrate—or at least accept—lifestyle and cultural differences
- Help preserve privacy
- Respect family rules
- Be patient
- Be accessible
- Follow through
- Don't become another layer of bureaucracy
- Be a partner
- Look at which services that families need, not whether they are billable (Dennis & Dennis, 2003)

Other Team Members

The composition of a Child and Family Team is extremely important. Some team members are prescribed by circumstance, such as the child's probation officer or child welfare caseworker. In addition, Karl and Kathy talk about inviting those people who know the child and family best from a positive point of view. For example, a teacher is good, but maybe the teacher who taught the child last year, who really liked him or her, is best. Besides the parents and the children, then, the Child and Family Team should include four to eight other people who best know the strengths and needs of the family. The family should choose these individuals, and the lead agency involved with the child and all members must agree to participate. Some examples of other possible members are:

- Teacher or counselor

- Social worker

- Probation officer

- Therapist

- Clergy

- Family friend or neighbor

- Foster parents

- Grandparents and other relatives (Dennis & Dennis, 2003)

Running the Child and Family Team

Karl and Kathy stress that the time and place for Child and Family Team meetings is crucial to their development and functioning. Meetings should be at times that allow all members to participate, which may include evenings and/or weekends. The concepts of family access, ownership and voice dictate that the meetings should take place where the family is comfortable. This may not necessarily be at home; some families may feel that a meeting in their home is too intrusive and might choose to meet at a neutral site, such as a house of worship.

The Child and Family Team meetings should be scheduled weekly for the first four weeks, monthly for the next several months, and quarterly thereafter. The spirit of individualized services leads to the conclusion that this schedule rarely happens as prescribed above. In reality, Karl and Kathy remind us, meetings need to be flexible in their scheduling, changing frequently to meet the family's needs or to respond to crises.

The team has a number of important jobs. Its role is to:

- assess family strengths;

- develop a plan for addressing needs;

- plan for crisis;

- develop a community support network to help implement the plan;

- advocate for the family;

- monitor the services and plan;

- evaluate the plan's effectiveness;

- redo the plan as needed...redo the plan as needed, redo the plan as needed...;

- be creative entrepreneurs; and,

- *Never, ever give up!* (Dennis & Dennis, 2003)

Life Domains

One essential aspect of Wraparound planning is the understanding that planning for families should not only include mental health issues, it must include issues in all areas of people's lives. Similarly, planning should not only focus on those areas of people's lives in which they have needs, but must include all areas of their lives—especially those areas in which they have particular strengths. The Community Partnership Group (1995), which was made up of John VanDenBerg, Mary Grealish, Pat Miles, and Neil Brown, talked about this Wraparound principle in terms of Life Domains. Although the group no longer exists, the concept of Life Domains has become part of the thinking on Wraparound. Generally, the Life Domains fall into the following areas:

- Living (or having a residence)

- Family

- Psychological/emotional (including psychiatric/medical)

- Educational/vocational

- Recreation/social

- Legal

- Spiritual

- Safety

- Health

One of the first tasks that a Child and Family Team must accomplish is for each family to define which particular domains are specific for their lives. One should not assume that everybody will see the domains of their life in the same way as others do. As an early part of the planning process, the team should identify strengths and needs for each of the life domains as defined by the family.

Crisis Planning

Effective crisis planning is one of the essentials of successful Wraparound. When children and adolescents come into care, it is usually because they have behaviors that create crises for their families and communities. For most of these youth, the nature of these crises is predictable. One of the main reasons children and youth fail in their homes and in formal placements is because they continue to do the same things that have created crises in the past, and as family members and professionals we continue to be surprised and disappointed each time it happens. Wraparound philosophy and practice accepts the fact that a youth has developed patterns of behavior in the past that he or she will continue to have in the present. Thus, when these behaviors happen, we should not be surprised. Rather, we should anticipate the crises and develop plans as to how we as a team, and others in the community who work with the child or youth, should deal with that crisis when it occurs.

The youth must be part of this crisis planning so that he or she becomes part of the solution as well as the problem. Instead of blaming a youth or family for a crisis when it occurs, the event should be used to help the team begin to see how predictable the youth's behavior is and to spark the team to think about new ways to help him or her avoid that behavior. Through this process, youth can then learn the nature of their problems and how to try and solve them on their own.

The Community Partnership Group (1995) created the following summary of the principles of crisis planning in Wraparound:

- Plan to anticipate crises based on past knowledge;

- Assume the worst-case scenario;

- Research past crises for cause and interventions and consequences that have worked the best;

- Clearly defined plans help teams function in difficult times;

- See crisis as a process with a beginning, middle, and end;

- Change the plan based on what works;

- Build plans that account for different levels of intensity and severity of crises;

- Build crisis plans early in the Child and Family Team's work;

- Begin by asking the family, "What can go wrong with this plan?";

- Always build in a 24-hour response;

- Clearly define roles for team members, including family and natural support people;

- Create time for the team to assess management of a crisis within two weeks of the event; and

- Decide that no major decisions or changes in the intervention plan will be made within 72 hours after a crisis event.

Principles for Success with Child and Family Teams

The work of the Child and Family Team has few rules, and there are many ways to approach the task. Beyond the advice in the earlier paragraph about defining life domains as an early task, we are uncomfortable prescribing a specific Child and Family Team process. Like everything else in Wraparound, the planning process must be individualized so that it both best meets the needs of the child and family and is comfortable for the professionals and other community participants. Although we will not prescribe any specific format to you, Karl and Kathy suggest some principles that should be part of whatever process you do come up with.

- Get to know the family

- Determine who team members should be

- Get an agreement from all members to participate

- Set up a meeting place and schedule

- Establish ground rules

- Assess strengths in all areas or life domains of the family

- Determine the percentage of needs currently met

- Brainstorm family and individual needs

- Prioritize needs

- Give parents veto power

- Match strengths with needs

- Assign task responsibility

- Develop a crisis plan

- Assess percent of needs that the plan is supposed to meet

- Track how well you are doing meeting the needs as you go along

- Set the date for the next meeting (Dennis & Dennis, 2003)

The process of a Child and Family Team is a dynamic one, thus it keeps changing. It has to, because, as we have presented over and over again in various chapters of this book, children, adolescents, and their families are constantly changing, as are their needs. The makeup of the Child and Family Team, with individuals who are close to and supportive of the youth and family, ensures that any planning that takes place is primarily geared toward meeting the needs of the youth and his or her family. At the same time, the Child and Family Team allows the youth and family to become part of any planning that has to take place to meet community needs, such as safety of the child and/or the community. The makeup of the team ensures that family's and the youth's strengths will not be overlooked, nor will the needs that the family sees as a priority, which may be in other life domains than the psychological. For example, the family may see a job for Dad as a more important need than access to outpatient psychotherapy or even behavioral control of the youth. The dynamic nature of the Child and Family Team and its inclusion of the family make it the ideal mechanism for bringing Wraparound to children, adolescents, and their families.

unnatural acts

Stories About Interagency Collaboration

There came a point in time that some of us who had been involved with Wraparound since its inception made the decision to formalize the Wraparound process. As the first part of that effort, we decided we needed to define what the basic elements of Wraparound were. We decided each of us would come up with our own list of elements and then we would get together and share the results. To our amazement, we all came up with basically the same list; what was really interesting was that the number one element which almost everyone had on their list was interagency collaboration. Now, this is unfortunate, because I have come to the opinion that interagency collaboration is an unnatural act between nonconsenting adults.

The reason for this is relatively simple—it's our education. If we go to school, we learn about our own specific discipline and service system, but there's very little cross-training that helps us understand the barriers and the advantages of other disciplines and systems. For example, if you have a master's degree in social work and are trained to work in child welfare, you probably are very good at what you do. Unfortunately, you most likely will not have had training in the field of education and will not really understand what a special education teacher does. If your background is in education, then you probably do that very well, but you really don't have a clue as to what a juvenile probation officer does, and, if your degree is in juvenile justice, you will not have a clue as to what a mental health specialist does.

Over time, most of us come to the conclusion that whatever service we are providing really makes sense and we feel we are doing a good job. But we are not so sure about the other guy, and we often feel the other service systems do not do as good a job as we do. The child welfare folks may think they do a great job, but the people in mental health may not agree, and vice versa. If you get child welfare and mental health together, however, they may well come to the joint conclusion that it's really education that is dropping the ball. If you get education to join the process with you, the job they are doing will suddenly look good, and the group will decide that it's really juvenile justice that's the culprit in this process. If juvenile justice also comes to the table with you, then everybody can agree that it is the private providers who are the problem. If you add the private providers to the mix, then everybody simply can agree, if these parents would just get their act together, then we wouldn't have all of these problems. In the end, we always seem to blame families!

Why is interagency collaboration important? There are several reasons. First, I believe that there are probably enough dollars in every community to provide the services to the children and adolescents who need it. The problem, however, is that the funds are tied up in services that are categorical, and those services always have stringent criteria for admission. For example, if you need to access the services provided by child welfare, you must have some issue of neglect or abuse in order to qualify for them. But once you get into the child welfare system, you may not automatically be entitled to any services you may need from mental health, special education, or juvenile justice. Likewise, if you have a learning disability, it may allow you to access the services of the education system, but not those of any other system. Each of our systems has certain, usually rigid, eligibility criteria for its interventions.

What happens when we start to blend those services across systems? If child welfare has 30 interventions, mental health has 30, juvenile justice has 30, education has 30, and we blend them together, then each individual and family who qualifies for any system is now looking at 120 services as opposed to only 30. This is one reason we believe interagency collaboration is very important.

When you bring systems together in an interagency process and you leave someone out, you have lost already, and you just do not know it. For example, suppose mental health, a private provider, and child welfare came together and put a wonderful plan together for a young person. Then in early September, representatives from these systems walk up to the school and say to the administrators there, "We've put together this great plan, and here is your part of it." The school is probably not going to get very excited about it. This is not necessarily because they are the education agency; it's because any system that is required to do the work but has not been part of the decisionmaking process is not going to get enthusiastic about providing those services.

Everybody needs to be part of the process. Since most of the children to whom we provide services have the most problems and are the hardest to serve, they will often be known to a minimum of two service systems, even three or four, so it is imperative that we pull each of these systems into the process.

When we first started creating interagency collaboratives, we only thought about including the human service providers: the people from child welfare, juvenile justice, special education, and mental health. We later started including private service-providing agencies, and finally, at one point, the parents became involved in the process, and very happily so. We were really pleased with how inclusive we had become, but we discovered that we had left out a very important community group: the movers and the shakers of the community, those people who control the culture and the direction of the community. Someone suggested that we bring those people into the interagency process because they would be great advocates. We need advocacy, because when the government changes every few years, the direction of public service delivery policy changes, too. If the last administration was centralizing services, the next one will want to decentralize those same services. When this occurs, the service level experiences a standstill for at least the first year or 18 months while the new administration is figuring out which direction to go in.

By involving community movers and shakers, they become a built-in advocacy group that can go to the new administration and say to them, "Look these services are a good thing, and they are something we need to continue with." We have seen the impact of advocates on a number of occasions. In one instance, as we were putting together a community team as part of a training, the team not only included the public agency people, but also people from the business community, the religious community, banks, real estate, and community action groups—the people who pretty much ran and controlled that particular community. As the meeting started, a person from one of the public agencies stood up and explained to the group what their mandate was, what services they provided, and what they could and couldn't do. He declared the limits of his agency's responsibility and what the responsibilities of some of the other public agencies in the group were. It was at that point the chair of the Chamber of Commerce stood up. He scratched his head and said, "I fail to understand why you people can't put all of these services together and work together on this." And he sat down.

The public agency representative was very patient with him. He once again explained to him why that could not occur. How the public agencies simply could not put it together because they all had certain criteria for services and certain limitations.

Again the Chamber of Commerce chair stood up and said, "It occurs to me that if the public agency leadership we have in this county cannot pull all these services together, then maybe we simply have the wrong leadership!"

The agency administrators needed to respond, and lo and behold, they started to explain how they could work together. The key here is, the community services do not belong to a handful of administrators, they belong to the entire community, and when you get the community leaders involved, they will help things to move in a more creative and positive direction.

Another time, one of our friends who is a tremendous community organizer had put together a community collaboration group that was doing very well. In the process, she discovered a video-store owner who had tremendous positive impact on some of the students from a nearby high school. She acted as an informal counselor. She would walk students back to school when they left early and, if they did their homework, she would give them free games. The students came to rely on her. She was so successful in working with them that our friend decided that the community needed to find a way to support her work. Unfortunately, the woman had an unsavory past. Nonetheless, our friend brought this lady to United Way to see if they would provide some additional dollars to help with her effort. The United Way folks got a little fidgety and informed the lady and our friend that they were not in the business of giving dollars to ex-prostitutes and ex-drug addicts.

Well, my friend went back and tried to figure out how she would make this work and remembered that one of the most powerful men in the community was a minister whom she knew. She went to him and explained her plight. The minister became convinced that this should be viewed as a mission for his church and he attended the next United Way meeting with the lady and our friend. At the beginning of the meeting, he stood up and said he would be very grateful to the United Way if they would make the decision to support his community by giving money to this woman who had been so successful in working with its youth, and he sat down. The people from the United Way then retired to confer. When they came back, they announced that not only were they giving her money, but they were going to give her more money than had been requested. The reason was very simple: the minister's advocacy had made it work.

We have seen some really positive results from the faith community being included on interagency collaboratives. In Houston, Texas' Third Ward, more than

100 houses of worship were identified as serving 25,000 people in that one community; each and every one of them provided some kind of service. As soon as leaders from some of those congregations were included in the interagency process, many of those services became known and available. As a result, they became useful for children in need who might not have had access to them before.

Another time, while doing a community assessment, we discovered that everyone involved felt that the one service missing was respite care for families, but that no funds for respite could be identified. At an interagency meeting, the person who was representing the ecumenical council said he would be willing to organize the rabbis and the ministers to recruit volunteers from their congregations to provide respite care. The representative from the mental health center offered to train those people who were to provide the respite service. The representative from a private provider agency that ran an active volunteer system agreed to structure and administer the process. As a result, they developed a respite system that was free of charge and that met the needs of many children and families in that community.

One of the best interagency efforts I was privileged to see was in Idaho. In the mid-1980s, I visited the state and spent time talking to a group of professionals about Wraparound and how it could change services. Afterwards, we went out to eat and have a few beers. After we had chatted for a while, one of the administrators from a very rural county said to me, "I don't know if this is what you mean and I don't know if we're doing it right, but I run the county educational system, and every Friday at three o'clock in the afternoon I meet with the heads of child welfare, juvenile justice, and mental health. We put together a list of problems that our families and children have for which we need to find additional services, and we beat our heads up against the wall until we come out with a plan. Because we do not have any money, we share the resources across systems in order to make things work. Is that what you mean?" And that was exactly what I meant.

In the late 1980s and early 1990s, as I did presentations, sometimes people would ask me how many communities or counties I could name that had really been successful in creating meaningful interagency processes, and I didn't have a very good answer for them. During that period, I had been involved with the federal Child and Adolescent Service System Program, which aimed to help states and communities create interagency approaches to serve the needs of children and adolescents with the most problems and their families. This project, CASSP, was started and run by Ira. I listened very seriously to Ira, who talked a lot about what made some communities work and what made others not work and looked for an opportunity to formulate some kind of study about that. In 1991, when Ira told me he was interested in looking at the 15 systems in the country that most people counted as being successful and trying to discover why, I got very excited. I couldn't think of anyone who was better qualified to do this than Ira, because I couldn't think of anyone who had been more intimately involved in this process and had traveled more and looked at more systems. So, I told him I thought this was such an important project that we, at Kaleidoscope, wanted to be part of it, and I volunteered to publish the monograph when he finished it.

Well, Ira did finish the monograph and Kaleidoscope published it, and it's still one of the best pieces of work on community systems and what makes them work that you can find anywhere. What became very clear to me from Ira's work is that to make services and systems effective, you must bring together into an interagency process those people who have the responsibility for providing the care. This thought confirmed many of the similar impressions I had come to working on Wraparound plans over the years. Ira focused primarily on the need for top-down services, or service policy driven by the highest-level state and community administrators. I have come to the further conclusion that, to be successful, services have to be not only top-down but also bottom-up, or driven by the families and the professionals who work with them day by day. Only those people who intimately feel the effects of service-delivery policy know how services need to be delivered. You cannot change the systems from the bottom alone, however. At the top, we need to have the people who run those agencies (or at the very least their second-in-commands), who are dedicated to working together on an interagency collaborative, dedicated to working with families, and dedicated to not only sharing power but sharing resources to make the process work. Of course, the best way to really determine if people are truly interested in collaboration is not only whether they come to the table, but whether or not they bring their resources or their money to the table as well.

How Interagency Systems of Care Came to Be

This part of the book should be the easiest for me to write. After all, as Karl alludes to in his stories, I spent a good part of my career at the National Institute of Mental Health (NIMH) working on how to create interagency systems of care at state and community levels. When I listen to Karl talk about his personal experiences with the need for community-level interagency teams, however, I gain a totally new perspective. You see, I came to my conclusions about the need for interagency teaming from my experiences working as the psychiatric consultant to a child welfare agency and during a short stint as the medical director of a community-based residential treatment center. I then spent the next several years of my career working at the federal level trying to find the answer to these interagency collaborative needs, finally helping to develop CASSP, which then became the concept I follow. CASSP was an administrative concept, created by federal bureaucrats and implemented by state bureaucrats. Although each of the people involved in the beginnings of the system of care had some clinical experience, at the time the program was developing, almost all of us had committed our lives to high-level administration. We had to hope that our efforts would lead to positive changes at the direct service-delivery level. Karl's stories tell us that they did. Not having a lot of experience getting interagency services for individual children and their families, my part of this chapter is not as easy for me to write as one might imagine.

Karl gives us lots of hints as to the various aspects of interagency collaboration that he feels are essential in the delivery of Wraparound services. In reality, his story in this chapter is more of a lecture on interagency collaboration in which he illustrates his points through experiences he has had working in various communities. You do not need another lecture on this topic from me; rather, I am going to thank Karl for talking about me in his story and use this opportunity to tell of how I came to recognize the need for community interagency teams; the development of CASSP at the National Institute of Mental Health, or NIMH, and its role in creating local interagency systems of care; and finally, some things I found out about in my study of local systems that Kaleidoscope published (1992).

When I finished my child psychiatry training in 1973, my first job was with NIMH. I was part of a special training program that NIMH had at that time called the Mental Health Career Development Program. Being part of this program allowed me to have some free time to explore areas of mental health while at the same time learning how to be a public health official. In my training, I had worked with one of the first child abuse teams in the country, the Trauma-X Team, at the Children's

Hospital of Boston, under the direction of Dr. Eli Newberger. When I got to NIMH, the federal government was in the middle of its first major child abuse initiative, and I was the guy who had just finished working in a model child abuse program. So, I became NIMH's Coordinator of Child Abuse Programs. This was a very exciting job, especially for a young doctor just out of training, and allowed me to meet many important and famous people in the field of child abuse and neglect; in addition, I was able to participate in the development of the government's new National Center for Child Abuse and Neglect. More importantly, I chose to use my free time to work as a consultant to the Montgomery County, Maryland, Department of Social Services' Child Protective Services Unit, which was in the building next door to my NIMH office. Not only did this work with Protective Services, as the unit called itself, allow me to augment the policy work I was doing in the field of child abuse and neglect with clinical experience, it also got me a free parking space in the Social Services parking lot, just outside the door to my NIMH office— a hot commodity at a huge federal building with insufficient parking. It was also a good deal for the Protective Service folks; they got a free child psychiatric consultant. In addition, because I worked as a bureaucrat rather than a full-time clinician, I was readily available when emergency evaluations needed to be performed, often within the hour.

I was fortunate that my connection with Protective Services offered me the opportunity to explore my own personal interest in adolescent psychiatry, and I was able to do some of the early work in the area of the abuse and neglect of adolescents. Most of all, my experience with child abuse and neglect services, especially as it pertained to adolescents, led me to some personal discoveries about the relationship between the child welfare and child mental health systems. As I worked with the Protective Services Unit, I also became available to the other units within that child welfare office that dealt with foster care, institutional placement, and in-home services. The more I worked with the child welfare population, the more clearly I saw how much the principles of that care and the principles of child mental health were similar. This should not have surprised me, given the history of child mental health as an outgrowth of child welfare and juvenile justice advocacy in the early 1900s, but it did.

I became convinced that it was impossible for the child welfare folks to do their jobs without some mental health input; however, that input was not readily available, and when available was not particularly responsive to the needs of the worker or the child in question. More than likely, the child welfare workers were also serving as mental health workers without even realizing they were doing it. I was not terribly disturbed by this; after all there is a fine line and a lot of crossover between clinical social work and casework training. I spent a lot of time trying to help the child welfare staff recognize and enhance their clinical impact, while at the same time trying to find them responsive, formal mental health resources that they could rely on in the community, in addition to myself. I was so convinced of the importance of the connection between child welfare services and mental health that I changed my federal job at NIMH–I moved from the part of the Institute that dealt with special populations (in my case, child abuse and alternative youth services) to the part that focused on the delivery of community mental health services through community mental health centers. I hoped to find ways of encouraging these centers to better integrate their services with their local child welfare services. I guess I was not very successful in doing that, and 25 years later we are still pretty much in the same place.

In my new job, I had an opportunity to expand my understanding of the relationship between community mental health services and the other child serving agencies. This was happening at the time when the federal government had become interested in the needs of a group of children and adolescents labeled as having serious (or severe) emotional disturbances, or SED. (I need to let you know that Karl despises this label, and prefers the term "emotionally unique" instead. I am going to use "SED" here because it is the term that most of the field uses; we don't always listen to Karl to the degree that we should–even I don't!) The interest in the population with SED followed from First Lady Rosalind Carter's personal interest in mental health service issues, which led to the creation of the President's Commission on Mental Health in 1978. The result of this commission was the development of an NIMH National Plan for the Chronically Mentally Ill. The Commission had found that the population of children and adolescents with SED was underserved, and the National Plan directed NIMH to do something about it. We child mental health folks at NIMH saw this finding as an opportunity to do more for child mental health services than we had ever been able to do before. As with most governmental initiatives, however, it had a slow start. A positive result of this for me was it gave me a chance to learn more about this population of children and adolescents with SED.

In 1981, I heard about a new facility in Montgomery County, Maryland, aimed at offering residential and day school treatment of children and adolescents with SED; it was called the Regional Institute for Children and Adolescents-Rockville, or RICA-Rockville. (I mentioned some of the lessons I learned while working at RICA in Chapter 5.) This was a new, model institution that had been open for a little more than one year. The concept of the program was that children and adolescents needed to be treated in their communities so that they could spend time and receive treatment within the context of their families and while integrated with the county school system. This facility had 80 beds, and another 100 day-school slots; almost all of the children and adolescents spent weekends home with their families. The school part of this facility was run by the county school system, and the students were often mainstreamed back into their home school as they got better.

RICA had had four medical directors in its first 18 months of operation. I had an opportunity to meet the latest of them as part of a consultation concerning one of the child welfare clients I had been working with who was now at this new program. This child psychiatrist mentioned to me how he had fallen into the position of medical director because the last guy had left precipitously and he had gotten stuck with the job; and like all of the three previous medical directors, he wanted out. I don't know if I am a masochist or if things at NIMH were so bad at that time that I just needed to get out any way that I could (you see, the Reagan administration had just come in and had wiped out the entire federal Community Mental Health Center Program for which I had worked, and we were all kind of depressed), but I pulled all the strings I could, and as part of my NIMH job, I got myself detailed to RICA as its medical director.

Now you have to understand that by this time in my career I had begun to recognize the principles that later became Wraparound, and as a result, had developed a fairly negative attitude toward residential placement of troubled children and youth. So my intention was to go to RICA as medical director and close it down. Of course, the first thing I learned there was that most of the young people had really serious problems and they needed to be in this residential form of treatment because the service alternatives required to keep them in the community were not available to help them. Since the RICA program was truly placed in the community and was family-oriented, I came to the conclusion that it was probably the best alternative possible for these children at that point in history (where is Kaleidoscope when you need it?). After a short time, I even became an advocate for the program—after all it was a good one. Within six months of leaving my position there and returning to NIMH, however, I was back to my original anti-residential treatment position. I guess absence does not always make the heart grow fonder.

The next thing I learned at RICA was more lasting for me, and I still use it as part of my training efforts. When I had been there only a few days, the Chief Executive Officer who ran the place told me that the statistics he had collected demonstrated that one-third of the young people had been referred from the child welfare system, one-third from juvenile justice and one-third directly from the school system. My first reaction to this was that none of them, or at most a handful, had come from the mental health system. Now, these were supposedly the children and youth with the most severe mental health problems, and they were not being served in anything called a mental health system—that was because there was none! Then I did some research of my own. I started to read the records of the young people in the program to find out how they had gotten there. I noticed several things. First, I saw that each of these children and youth carried with them huge records, often more than a foot thick. As I looked through those records, I noticed that few, if any, of the young people had had adequate mental health treatment. Few had ever had a good evaluation, and for those who had, the recommendations of that evaluation had not been implemented.

My second reaction was that, as I got to know the children in the program, I could not tell from knowing them and their behavior and progress in the program which of the service systems they had come from. It seemed to me that there was no relationship between the kinds of problems and emotional symptoms a child or youth had and the service system in which he or she ended up. More often there were situational, family, economic, and/or even racial bias factors that determined whether they ended up in the child welfare, juvenile justice, or special education system.

Another set of thoughts struck me later in my stay at RICA. These had to do with what happened when the children and adolescents who had been at RICA were ready to leave the institution's programs. When they left, they needed to find noninstitutional services elsewhere in the community. Some needed to go home, but needed intensive in-home services. Some needed to go into less intensive residential programs, such as therapeutic group homes and therapeutic foster care. But some of these programs were run or paid for by child welfare, some by juvenile justice, and none by mental health. This meant that if you were a RICA student who had been placed there by the schools as part of special-education plan, and you needed a group-home kind of placement, you probably couldn't get it, because most of the group homes were funded by child welfare and juvenile justice, and you were most likely not eligible for care under either of those systems. It seemed that there was no way to provide care as good as that provided by RICA in the community under the administrative and funding systems that were in place. They were lacking an interagency mechanism, and coordinated care was almost impossible to obtain.

All of my experiences at RICA taught me that there were lots of good programs in communities, and if you were able to get yourself into one of these, you probably could get appropriate care. In addition, it became clear that if you had a simple need that could be taken care of alone in one of the major child-serving systems like child welfare, juvenile justice, education, or mental health, you could probably get that care. But as soon as you had multiple needs, it was difficult, if not impossible to find the proper care. Because of our multiple funding streams and referral bases at RICA, we were in a position to meet children's multiple needs while they were there. But as soon as those young people left RICA, they were thrown back into a fractionated situation where they had limited access only to those services for which they qualified on the basis of the agency that had referred them to RICA in the first place. (It is strange that I learned this valuable lesson about the power of interagency community funding while working in an institution!) Two major consequences followed from the lack of interagency mechanisms in the community. In the better of the two, some stayed at RICA longer than they needed to so that they could be discharged when they were well enough to use the particular programs available to them under the public service system to which they were connected. The worse scenario saw others leaving RICA after a profitable stay, only to flounder and/or fail in the community because the services appropriate for their needs were not available to them.

After my stay at RICA, I returned to NIMH, where I was given the opportunity to create a new federal program for the population of children and adolescents with SED. What emerged was CASSP, which was built around all of the problems I had learned about at RICA in helping families obtain the services needed by their children and youth with SED. Primary among those problems was the lack, in most communities, of an interagency process to facilitate this type of care.

CASSP was a program that was also based on several of the premises that Karl talked about. The program's first, but unspoken goal, was to have a person at the state level in every state and the District of Columbia whose sole responsibility was child mental health services. Less than half the states had such a person in 1984, when CASSP began. (CASSP reached that goal in seven years, but, after the federal CASSP grant funds faded out, some states have lost that capacity.) The formal goals of CASSP were based on four realities: children with the most serious problems needed an interagency approach; very few mental health services were available to these youth; care needed to be delivered in a culturally competent manner; and, families needed to be an important part of their children's care.

First, the children with the most serious emotional problems very often needed care from more than one of the large public service agencies for children: child welfare, juvenile justice, special education, and, of course, mental health. As I mentioned before, I had learned when I worked at RICA that the children and youth who ended up in the most intensive treatment settings had multiple needs but were only getting part of those needs met, usually those that related to the public service system they had fallen into: child welfare, juvenile justice, or special education. When these youth got to the treatment center, it was impossible for me to tell which of them came from which of these systems. Not to say that they "all looked alike," but rather, each of these youth had a unique set of needs, and because of one incident at a point in time, they had ended up in one system or another. Each child had needs that required services from several systems. All the youth had mental health needs; that situation defined why they were there. Each had educational needs; of course, all young people have educational needs, but some of them have special-education needs. Many of the youth came from families who needed services provided by child welfare. Similarly, many youth had had brushes with the law and were connected to the juvenile justice system. Yet most of them had been identified as "belonging" to only one system, and when they did get services from another system, it occurred in an uncoordinated manner. These youth had interagency needs, and it was clear that they needed to have those needs met through an interagency process.

Second, CASSP recognized that necessary mental health services were not readily available to the children and adolescents with the greatest needs. As I stated in regards to the residential treatment center, there is no formal mental health system for children and adolescents in most communities. It became a goal of CASSP to increase the resources going to child mental health and to increase the presence of a child mental health system so that it could be as equally useful as the child welfare, education, and justice systems. Most states and communities do not have a public mental health system for children. States themselves rarely provide direct mental health services, with the exception of some state hospital services, but rather offer access to those services through their Medicaid and community mental health center programs. Neither of these mechanisms ensures adequate or appropriate child mental health services.

Third, CASSP moved toward the delivery of more culturally competent services. When CASSP started, it was clear that a very high percentage of children and adolescents who utilize publicly financed children's services were from various minority groups, and that if we were going to be effective, we needed to make sure that the special needs of these minority groups were considered in the development of service systems. I didn't have any idea how to make this happen. So CASSP brought together a committee of folks from various minority groups for the purpose of telling us how to do this. They were a very effective group and did their job well, basically creating and defining the concepts of cultural competence. The group nominated four individuals to write a monograph spelling out the nature of this concept and how it needed to be applied to a system of care for children and adolescents with SED. Karl was one of these four, along with Terry Cross, Mareasa Isaacs, and Barbara Bazron. (You might remember Karl's story from Chapter 8 on Cultural Competence, about how Mareasa, Barbara, and he, all African Americans, learned an important lesson in cultural competence themselves from Terry, who is an American Indian, as they worked on this monograph.)

Last, but certainly not least, CASSP aimed at more meaningful inclusion of families in the care of their children and in the development of the local and state service systems under which they were to obtain care. As a psychiatrist, the need for this was not particularly evident to me at first. I did feel that families were important to include in the CASSP process, but not for the reasons that you might imagine, given the content of this book and my commitment to family involvement in the care of their children. At first, my interest in including family members in CASSP was for them to serve as advocates. You see, I was very much impressed with the history of child mental health and the fact that, over the last 100 years, there had been a number of advocacy movements for better and more available mental health services. I was impressed with the success each of these movements had had at the time they were in force; I was also impressed with the fact that each of them had come and gone without much, if any, follow-through. When I first started working at NIMH, one of my first jobs was with a federal Child Advocacy Program that had been started in response to a large national child advocacy effort called the Joint Commission on the Mental Health of Children which published an important report in 1970. (My father, Reginald Lourie, was the chairman of the Joint Commission, so I felt very close to it.) NIMH had participated in the funding of a number of Child Advocacy Projects as its part in supporting the findings of the Joint Commission; one of my jobs, from 1973 to about 1975, was to monitor some of these projects. Although they were truly exciting, when I had the opportunity to work with CASSP only ten years later, almost nobody had any memory of these projects, even in the states where they had been funded.

I saw CASSP as the next child advocacy project, and I didn't want it to be forgotten in ten years. In addition, at the time we were developing CASSP, NIMH had a new project called the Community Support Project, or CSP. This project had been started about seven years before CASSP, and its goal was the creation of community responses for adults with severe and persistent mental health problems. CSP had helped to create an organization of parents of these chronically mentally ill adults and had acted as an advocate for services and research for this population and for CSP itself. This organization, the National Alliance for the Mentally Ill, NAMI, became a huge force in making sure that CSP and the population it served were not to be forgotten. I felt there needed to be such support for children's services as well, and that a similar child-oriented parent organization was necessary to assure that any gains made under the new CASSP effort would continue.

This lesson was driven home to me once when a Congressional committee held a hearing on child mental health issues. Congressional committee hearings work like this. In a large room, there is a huge dais where the Congressional committee members sit. Behind them sit their aides, who know the issues well, provide questions for the Congressmen to ask and take notes. Usually, only one or two particularly interested committee members attend the hearing. On this occasion, there were to be two panels of individuals presenting to the committee. The first panel was made up of professionals who had been involved with system-of-care efforts related to CASSP. True to form, only one Congressman was there to listen, and he appeared less than interested. When the second panel, made up entirely of parents of children and adolescents with mental health problems arrived to present, however, the dais was filled with committee members, each of whom not only appeared interested, but also had questions they wanted to ask of the assembled panel of family members.

My partner in the development of CASSP, Judith Katz-Leavy, took on the task of assembling a group of family members to support our program. The first thing these parents taught me was that they were not there to support *my* program; rather, they had come to help create *their* program. They had to beat me up a bit before I got the message, but once I did, we formed a powerful alliance of professionals and family members who advocated together for the types of programming that best met the needs of their children. At this point, some 20 years later, I have trouble telling who among my CASSP colleagues are family members, professionals, or both—we have all become knowledgeable partners in making child mental health services relevant and effective.

I left the federal government in 1991, seven years after the initiation of CASSP. At that time, the program had successfully created a national movement to foster and provide more meaningful, coordinated services for the population of children and adolescents with SED and their families, and had met its goal of affecting every state in the Union. One of the reasons I left my NIMH position was that I was tired of being a bureaucrat, although I had enjoyed the experience that that part of my career had afforded me in terms of having an impact through making things happen. The downside to that type of career was that other people are out doing lots of exciting work, while I was sitting in an office in Rockville, Maryland, encouraging and enabling them to do that work. By that time, I wanted the opportunity to do some of the exciting work myself. The first thing I wanted to do when I left NIMH was to embark on a study of local system development. Having seen success in creating interagency processes at the state level, I wanted to figure out how this was being translated and practiced at the local level and to begin to understand what the ingredients were for the development of a well-functioning local interagency system of care.

I have to admit that this study was not very scientific. I chose the sites I was to visit by asking people I knew around the country where the best functioning local systems of care were. I was interested in the State of Missouri because they were trying out variety of interesting models in various communities around the state. The Missouri Institute of Mental Health was also interested in this and became one of the primary funders of the study. In addition, I visited some communities that had received grant money from the Robert Wood Johnson Foundation's Mental Health Services Program for Youth, which had funded 10 community system-of-care efforts based on the principles of CASSP in cities around the country. The Foundation supported my visits to two of their sites. Other sites came to me by word of mouth, and the National Institute of Mental Health funded my visits there.

This study taught me a number of very interesting things. Most importantly, it taught me that creating an interagency process in a community is neither an easy nor a short-term project. In the communities I visited that were the most successful by my measures, it was clear that the interagency process had been developing for a number of years, usually more than five, and often as much as ten. In these successful communities, the process had often begun when two or three like-minded individuals who had worked in the various public child-serving agencies got together informally to discuss the problems they were having in making sure that children and adolescents with complicated problems and their families obtained the services that they needed. At that time, Wraparound services were not readily available in most communities, and these folks were struggling to make sense out of the service systems in their localities. As they talked together, they had discovered that they all had a similar picture of how difficult it was for these youth and their families to obtain meaningful services. Together they had come to the same conclusions that if service were to be delivered in a more useful way, they would have to work together. I saw this "coming together" as the creation of what I called a "shared vision." And it is this shared vision that allowed the leaders in these communities to find a purpose to bring their services together into a single interagency service system.

In my study, the individuals were most often leaders of the various child-serving public agencies, such as mental health, child welfare, juvenile justice, and/or special education. It was not usually the directors of these agencies (even though in some instances it was), but more than likely it was somebody at the level just below the director. I think these people have more flexibility to express their ideas than directors do because the director is often a political appointee who has to reflect the official agency or community policy, and the individuals at the next level down are often more free to innovate. Of course, they do need the blessing of their bosses before they can participate in the interagency process. Others, such as family members and other advocates, are often part of this group of individuals who share a common vision.

While having a shared vision was an important first step in the formation of a local interagency service system, vision alone was not enough to make it happen. Someone among these individuals with the shared vision needed to lead in order for the process to move ahead. In some communities, it was one individual who took the initiative to move the group's shared vision into a formal interagency process; in other cases, it was several individuals who took a leadership initiative together. Regardless, I found in communities that had been successful that ultimately, the original leader or leaders had given up sole leadership to a larger group, which then became a leadership group. The power of these groups was the force that pushed the development of the local interagency process.

Still, shared vision and leadership alone were not sufficient to allow the creation of an interagency system of care. In every community I visited and studied, some event or project came along that acted as a catalyst which the leadership group took advantage of to get momentum for their efforts. I call these catalysts, or trigger mechanisms. In one community, a judge who got angry at the lack of coordination of service for a particularly difficult-to-serve youngster gave the leadership group a reason to put their shared vision into action. In another community, the failure of one of the local public agencies to obtain state certification was the impetus for a well-respected community service leader to bring together all of the agencies into one single system. In yet other communities, it was state-driven interagency projects, such as local CASSP efforts, that offered the leaders in those places an opportunity to actualize their vision.

Often, it takes more than one trigger mechanism to get things rolling. In the community that originally started their efforts in response to the angry judge, they also applied for a state interagency system-of-care demonstration grant. The process of writing the grant acted as a trigger mechanism that brought them together in a more formal way. Even though they didn't get the grant, they created their system anyway. They applied again at the next opportunity and they further developed their system, but they still didn't get the grant. By the time they actually did get the grant, their system was well in place and the grant monies were used to help solidify the interagency gains they had made. The important aspect of those communities that used more than one trigger mechanism is that they used each mechanism to build on the last one(s). In many communities, when they get a new grant they start in a new direction based on the content of that grant. In the successful communities that I studied, they did something else; they put each new grant effort together with the last one, making each new trigger mechanism build on the last, toward their shared vision.

I believe that these three principles—shared vision, leadership, and trigger mechanisms—are the basics of local system development. Without them, no community will be able to develop a community-wide interagency system of care. In addition, it became apparent in the study that time was another important factor. Shared vision and leadership take time to develop in a community, often a decade or more. This is more likely to happen in a less urban community, because the potential leaders tend to stay in their jobs longer and have more opportunity to interact with each other to share their visions. Time is essential for trigger mechanisms to appear so that the leaders can take advantage of them. Time is also necessary as the leaders work to help other potential leaders in vital positions to accept the shared vision and join in the development of the local interagency process.

While my study did find out a number of other things about successful local system development, I will only talk about one other. I studied communities of all sizes, from ones serving as few as 90,000 people (about 30,000 in a small city and the rest in surrounding county or counties), to large urban centers serving over a million people. As I examined and charted my data, I discovered that the optimal population size among the sites that I visited was about 225,000. I have come to explain this phenomenon by thinking that larger populations create a service need that is too large to manage. The public children's service agencies are huge and have trouble controlling themselves. In the smaller sites, the agencies are smaller, reflecting the size of the population in need, and as a result are more manageable. The smaller sites tended to have fewer funding resources, however, and as a result, fewer service options available for children and their families. When the population of a community is around a quarter of a million, there seems to be a perfect mix. The agencies are small enough so that they are workable and the communities are large enough so they can afford to support the full range of services necessary to meet families' needs.

This is probably more than most readers ever wanted to know about interagency development. It is important to understand how difficult it really is to bring it about, however. While Karl's stories demonstrate to us how important and powerful interagency collaboration at the community level is in supporting the development and practice of Wraparound service delivery, we must keep reminding ourselves how hard these interagency processes are to get started and to maintain. The lesson that Karl and I bring to you is that if you want to use a Wraparound process to help your family or others in your community, you must pay attention to the development of an interagency system of care in that community. It will not happen naturally or by itself. If you do not or cannot do it, someone else must.

chapter eleven

never pay for anything you can get for FREE

Stories about Cost-Effective Services and
Outcome Measurement

Never pay for anything that you can get for free! At Kaleidoscope, we believe this—not because we are cheap, but because we feel our job is to work our way out of a job. One of the ways we do this is to find services that are available for people in the community. On one occasion, I was observing a California group put together a Wraparound plan when something happened that disturbed me. Part of the plan being developed for this young person was to get him a computer, and the team had set aside funds to buy it. Now, it seemed to me that if you live in Silicon Valley, where they make all of the computers, the last thing you need to *buy* as part of a service plan is a computer! You should be able to find someone in one of those computer companies who will donate one—not only donate the computer but also agree to keep it upgraded and running. This way, when you are no longer there, a relationship will still exist between the person who has the computer and the company that provided it. At Kaleidoscope, we put a lot of thought into the concept of cost-effectiveness over the years, and we came to discover the power of informal services and how cost-effective they can be. We thought it was obvious that getting a free computer would allow you to have more money available to pay for some other service for that youth that you couldn't get for free, or to buy a service for another youngster for whom a free service is not available.

Another time, during a Wraparound training in Cheyenne, Wyoming, I had a conversation with a young social worker in which I said, "I think it is important that every time you are out in your community visiting an establishment such as a convenience store, a restaurant, or a bowling alley, you should ask the people who run those businesses if they might be willing to help some of the people you serve by extending them some of their products or services. A long time ago, I came to the conclusion that if you ask the people who run the bowling alley for money, they will probably run like hell! But, if you ask, 'Can I have a few lanes for a family in need?', you are more likely to get that. You might ask the owners of a restaurant, 'Would you be willing to allow for a dinner for a family once a week?', or a beauty shop owner, 'Would you be willing to do someone's hair?', or a clothing store owner, 'Would you be willing to share some of last year's styles, donating them to families in need?' If you ask these kinds of questions, you will be amazed at what you can get. We discovered that people are really interested in helping others, but they find it much easier to provide products or services than money."

I went on to tell her about how my favorite example of this came to pass at Kaleidoscope. "For years, we had been attempting to get a monetary donation from one of the most incredibly wealthy banks in Chicago. In response to our pleas, we always got the nicest letters back from them—however, they all said 'No!' Our new director of development came up with an interesting idea that led us to take another tack. She went to visit one of that bank's officials, and together they implemented her simple plan. Kaleidoscope would create an information card about each person we were serving, which listed the person's first name, age, and a list of three things they wished to get for Christmas. The bank's role was to offer these cards to its employees, each of whom could then choose a person's card and buy them the Christmas gifts they wanted. As a reward, the bank held a Christmas reception for those employees who had chosen to participate; they would bring their gifts to the reception, and later, we would deliver them to the families. One year, this bank's employees donated 1,700 Christmas gifts!

"After we had done this for several years, something really interesting began to happen. Many of the bank employees would pick the same people every year as the recipient of their gifts. After this had gone on for a while, some of these bank employees began to become more interested in the individuals for whom they had been buying gifts. They would ask questions such as, 'When is this child's birthday?' or 'Do they need some help to graduate from school?' You see, they wanted to participate more deeply with those families—even though they never ever really knew who they were. The most touching thing I heard at one of those receptions was the personal story told by one of the employees. She related how she had been raised in a relatively poor environment and how this experience made her feel that giving was part of what people needed to do. Every Christmas, she would pick up a number of the cards and give one of them to each of her children, each of whom was to take the responsibility for doing the shopping for that family. She said that she used this experience as a lesson to teach them how important it was to give and to share things with other people."

Finally, I told this social worker in Cheyenne, "If you look into your community, you, too, will be able to find people who will assist."

Most people make the assumption that it is easier find free resources in a large city like New York, Chicago, or Los Angeles, because they think there are many more resources there. But the reason I chose to tell you about this particular conversation with the social worker from Cheyenne, Wyoming, (a city with a little over 50,000 people), is that I went back there three months later and discovered this same social worker had taken my words to heart and had found 29 free services in that community. It can be done in any community, but you have to look, and you have to ask!

Another issue concerning cost-effectiveness for Wraparound is that if we keep children at home with their families, put them into their own apartments, or move them into treatment foster care as opposed to residential programs, institutions, and hospitals, the costs plummet. When we keep young people out of institutions, we do not have to pay for bricks, mortar, and maintenance to build and keep those systems going. Institutional cost is one of the things my Wraparound colleagues from around the country and I talk about, and as a group, we agree that none of us has ever been in a state that is not supporting some children at a $1,000 a day! On the other hand, there is no one that I'm aware of who can even spend $1,000 a day on a Wraparound plan. Wraparound is by nature always cost-effective and is much less expensive than other types of service delivery that we provide.

Once I was putting together a Child and Family Team for a mother at a psychiatric hospital. As we started, one of the helping people came in with Mom and immediately said, "We can't do this Wraparound today because we have a crisis!"

I asked, "What is this crisis?"

The worker said, "The crisis is that she's been evicted! She has to be moved out of her house within three days, so what we have to do is to look for an apartment for her."

"Have you had any success at all, and how long have you been looking?" I asked.

He replied, "We've been looking for two weeks and we've been unable to find an apartment for her."

So, I asked the people assembled there, "Is there anyone in the room who knows someone in real estate?"

Three or four people, I can't remember exactly how many, raised their hands and said, "Yes."

I said, "Would one of you do me a favor and go out to the telephone and see if one of your contacts can get an apartment for this young lady?"

One of them went out and came back in a few minutes with four possibilities of apartments—two of which were certainties. The point of this story is that many times when we only use those individuals who are directly working with a family in the process of finding services for them, we miss a lot of resources that other people in the community might know about. The smaller the number of people we include in a helping network, the less likely we are to reach out to informal services. We need to develop and use our own networks in order to best find help for the people that we serve.

Once, as members of an assessment team looking at a mental health system in a community, Ira and I were responsible for looking into the local hospital and coming up with some suggestions that might be useful in making it more community-oriented. To our horror, the first thing we discovered was that there was a 4-year-old on the children's ward of this hospital! Given our understanding that the admission criteria for this public hospital included "being a danger to one's self or others," we asked on what basis this 4-year-old had been hospitalized. To our shock, we were told he was "homicidal." What this really meant was that he had gone after his mother with a butcher knife. We didn't quite understand why she hadn't just reached out and taken the knife away from him. But, the more we talked to the staff of the hospital, the more we realized the real problem here was that they had not been out into the community looking for an appropriate placement for this child, whether it was with his family or whether it was with someone else in the community. As a result, he was stuck on the psychiatric ward at age 4. Also on that ward was a 12-year-old who was in full restraints! He too had been admitted because he had been deemed homicidal. While he did seem to be a bit "hyper," he did not appear very dangerous, and after exploring his history, it seemed to us that some other things could have been done to help him other than to put him in the hospital—with or without restraints.

As part of the discussion during this site visit, we discovered the hospital grounds themselves held a major unused resource. We found four or five cottages on the property that seemed to be in reasonably good condition. One of our suggestions was that until the hospital could find a way to place these children back home or in the community, it would certainly be more humane, as well as more cost effective, for one or more of those cottages to be furnished and staffed so some of those hospitalized children could be placed in a more home-like setting. Often, the solution to saving money and the solution to providing more humane services is simply just to look around us to see what is available.

The cost is only one part of being cost effective; providing effective services is the other. Part of having a cost-effective approach is to figure out whether what you are doing for somebody is working or not. To do this, it is important that evaluation be part of any Wraparound process. These evaluations must make sense and be constructed so that they help the program do better work, however. Several things have disturbed me about most of the evaluations that have been done with Wraparound. The first of these is the number of years it takes to do them. Any good program is constantly evolving, and if you are doing it right, you shouldn't be doing the same thing today that you were doing three years ago. So if we do an evaluation that takes three years to complete, then part of that evaluation tends to be useless. I think this tells us that evaluations need to be done more quickly and be more to the point with faster feedback. In this way the evaluation will be measuring what really happened rather than assuming things were static. Furthermore, the people who are running and doing the work of the program might be able to benefit from the information that comes out of the evaluation.

Second, a lot of evaluations are written in a scientific language that no one can read except for other evaluators. Evaluations need to be written in such a way that they can be used to educate those people in the community who have the power to make our programs thrive, such as judges, politicians, or agency heads. Evaluations need to be in language that these non-mental-health professionals can understand—that can help them know what we are talking about. Evaluations that people cannot understand are useless to them and us.

Third, I hate evaluations that measure things that don't matter. I am not really interested in whether or not you have raised someone's "self-esteem." There are things to measure that make a lot more sense, such as behavior. For example, if a young person had been truant from school 30 days last year, and was only truant 10 days this year, then, evidently, we are moving in the right direction. If a child had been hospitalized 20 days last year, and only 5 days this year, again we are moving in the right direction. Here is another such measure—one judges do not seem to like: if a youth stole six cars last year, and only one car this year, we are probably moving in the right direction. These are the kind of things I like to measure. It would be better if we did not measure individuals or families against somebody's concept of what the community standard might be; rather, we should measure people's performance against how well they have done in the past, before they participated in the Wraparound process, or in any other intervention process.

One last thing about the measurement of outcomes is the effect that Wraparound has on a community. We need to measure the amount of money we are saving by not sending these children to out-of-community facilities. We also should know how many jobs we have created by keeping people at home in their own communities. Although these kinds of data are not often examined, this is the kind of information that community leaders could use to help support Wraparound in their communities.

Why Wraparound is Cost-Effective and Outcome-Oriented

When I first started writing my notes for this chapter, I was annoyed. "Why should we have to focus so heavily on cost-effectiveness?" I mumbled. "Why isn't the value of Wraparound just assumed? I've never had to justify the cost of any other intervention!" I wrote the phrase, "In an ideal world, cost-effectiveness would not be an issue." Then I took a step back and asked the question, "If it were just a matter of justifying Wraparound, why would cost-effectiveness be listed as one of its underlying principles?" And I thought, "Maybe there is something more basic about cost-effectiveness than finding free stuff and justifying the service through positive outcomes?" My commentary for this chapter will explore this question and then go on to talk about some of my ideas about measuring outcomes.

A few years ago, I had the opportunity to do a study of innovative services that were becoming available to families who paid for their services on their own and/or with private health insurance. One of the findings that came out of that study was that managed care, along with its cost-effectiveness, could be seen as one of those innovations. The reason this was true was that an underlying principle of good managed care is to get the right amount of the right service to an individual and/or family at the right time, for the right amount of time. Although there are lots of reasons why current managed care practice does not live up to this principle (they will not be a subject for this book on strength-based approaches), managed care has become popular in the health business because it is extremely cost-effective based on its practice of careful monitoring of services and needs and the attempt to match them up.

As I was writing up the findings for this study, I had a realization that this principle of ideal managed care was similar, if not identical, to what I saw as a basic principle of Wraparound. Chapter 9, on Child and Family Teams, focuses on the role of the team in determining what specific interventions and services a child and his or her family need at any moment in time. As I wrote this chapter, I came to realize that this concept was in reality a most important lesson in the Wraparound principle of cost-effectiveness.

Let us take a look at this principle by asking the question, "Do better efficiency and better service go together?" Well, I'm not sure that efficiency is what we strive for. What we strive for is the best, most appropriate service we can offer to a family. The job of the Child and Family Team is to do just that. As they measure the strengths and needs of a family, they decide what services, formal and informal, can be brought to bear on behalf of the family—many times that family will even provide some of the informal services itself. The service package is arranged, not because it is what is available (whether or not it fits the need) or because it is cost-efficient; rather, it is because it makes the most sense. If there are free, informal services that can be utilized, great! They work well mostly because they are the services that make most sense, regardless of the cost. If a formal, more costly service were the best alternative, that is what should be used. There is another side to this, however. One of the functions of the Child and Family Team is to continually monitor the applicability of each service and the progress made in using it. When a particular service is no longer necessary, the Child and Family Team discontinues it. If that service is not working for the child or family, then another, more effective service is found. In this way, the child and/or family only use the services they need at any particular moment in time.

Such is not the case when using traditionally planned and delivered services. In this traditional scenario, a treatment planning team looks at the needs of the child and family and comes up with a list of recommended services. Usually, they only recommend formal categorical services. The trouble with categorical services is that they only serve some people well. In other words, if you fit in, the service may work well for you. If you don't fit in, the service will most likely not have the capacity to bend itself to meet your special needs, and it usually won't work very well for you. Wraparound has the capacity to make sure that any service that it recommends for a child and family is tailor made; therefore, it has a much better chance of fitting well. Wraparound offers the capacity to add something extra to a categorical service to make it fit better and therefore more useful, when without that add-on that categorical service might not be so effective. To offer someone a categorical service that does not fit his or her needs and therefore dooms him or her to failure is not very efficient. To put someone in a categorical service that has been modified so that it fits better is much more efficient. Finding the perfect fit of a service to a need is most likely to engender success, and is therefore very efficient. It is like buying a pair of slacks. If you buy the wrong size, you will spend a lot of extra time trying to adjust them. If you buy them too long, you may trip on them and/or wear out the cuffs, and they won't last as long. If you buy them the wrong size and have them altered, they may cost a little more, but you will be much less likely to trip over them. If you buy individually tailored slacks, they often don't cost much more, and they will fit better. Any slacks that you buy will be better for you if you alter them when you change size. Much too often, traditional categorical programs come either as one-size-fits-all, or as "All we have left are extra large and extra small...take your pick."

One example of the former are those school-based programs where children are placed for a semester or a whole school year, whether they need a shorter or longer period of time. Although there are often well-stated justifications for a program's set time period, it is still very inefficient and can get in the way of a child's progress. The most common recent example of "too small" is the practice by which managed care companies dole out a services based on a preset authorization (such as 10 or 12 outpatient therapy visits) that is determined out of context of the child, family, and/or Child and Family Team.

I hope this discussion has led the reader to the conclusion that truly individualized services are, by nature, more efficient. Maybe that is how the Wraparound principle should really be described—just plain "efficient," rather than "cost efficient." The discussion also reminds us that the Child and Family Team is the most important vehicle for making the Wraparound process efficient. This efficiency is enhanced by the use of nontraditional and noncategorical services. That is because they fit the need better. It just so happens that many of these services are informal and/or free. In a traditional system, we do not always utilize informal services. The rationale for this is often tied up in issues of accreditation and confidentiality. When we deny ourselves the opportunities offered by informal services, we make our care less efficient.

Outcomes are one way to track how well the intervention as recommended by the Child and Family Team is doing. Many folks get freaked out by the concept of outcomes. They think of them as something that only evaluators and researchers can measure, and furthermore, they tend to think of them as things that have the capacity, and maybe the prime purpose, of reducing funding. In reality, that is not the story. We all measure outcomes all the time. In our daily lives, we measure lots of outcomes. "How did that recipe turn out? Should I use it again? Did it get me kudos, or did it make someone sick?" In our work with young people, whether we are parents or professionals, we constantly measure how well our approaches work. Most of us have developed our approaches to parenting and professional intervention through trial and error. "I'll try this. If it works, I'll try it again; if it doesn't, I'll try something new." These are all outcomes that we measure informally as our personal and professional lives proceed.

If we accept this definition of "outcome," then we can see that the Child and Family Team in a Wraparound process is measuring the outcome of its plans on an ongoing basis. Each member of the team—family or professional—is doing a daily assessment of how things are going. From this assessment, the plan is amended as needed. The team continues to use what works (has a positive outcome) as long as it is working. When something doesn't work (makes no difference or has a negative outcome) the team discontinues it and tries something else. As the young people say, "Duh!" Outcome measurement is a basic concept that underlies the Wraparound principle of efficiency.

So, why all of this fuss about cost-effectiveness and outcomes? This is the political part that leads us to worry about cost-efficiency. It is a political reality that change doesn't come easily, and when we do something new, like Wraparound, we are asked to prove that it works. Never mind that Wraparound has a built-in assurance that it will work, through its focus on efficiency and outcomes. Somehow, old things, like residential treatment (which has proven over and over again to be inefficient, with high costs and poor outcomes) never seem to have to prove themselves. As a newer service-delivery model, Wraparound is under a microscope. Therefore, we need to formalize our outcome measurement and prove our cost-effectiveness, over and over again.

The good news is that we are lucky. Most of the research on Wraparound services has demonstrated that it is less expensive than traditional approaches. Probably the most famous of these was the first major state use of Wraparound—the Alaska Youth Initiative (AYI), which Karl discussed in the first chapter. AYI's aim was to bring back to Alaska those youth who had been sent out of state for care for their emotional problems, some of whom were costing state agencies nearly $200,000 a year. The theory for making this happen was to take the money that was already being spent on each of these children and apply it to buying them care in Alaska. The state brought in Karl and Mel Breed from Kaleidoscope to teach them the principles of Wraparound so that they could be used in developing intervention plans for each of these youth. To demonstrate how this type of approach could work, think of any youngster you know who has unique and hard-to-serve needs and imagine what kind and how much service you could buy for that youngster if you had $200,000 a year to spend on him or her, or even $100,000, or $60,000, or $50,000. Then imagine how wonderful it would be to be given the authority to buy anything you and the Child and Family Team felt would help that child. In the Alaska Youth Initiative, they bought things as interesting as a snowmobile for one child (I forget the justification for that).

What they found in Alaska was that for the first six months, they were spending money for each child at pretty much the same rate that had previously been spent buying residential treatment; however, after that first six months, the costs dropped down sharply. Did the costs stay down, you ask? For the most part, they did. During certain periods of time (sometimes a few days and sometimes a few months), the state did have to spend more. But, because this was Wraparound, the Child and Family Team was able to control the use of more intensive and costly services so they were only used when absolutely necessary, and they were able to stop using the high-intensity services the moment they were no longer necessary, thus keeping the costs relatively low.

The other thing they did in Alaska was to anticipate that if you gave a Child and Family Team a lot of money to spend on a child and family, you better be able to both justify the use in the first place and demonstrate that there was a positive outcome. To do this was relatively simple. First, they gave the Child and Family Teams the job to document the reasoning they used to make their decisions to buy any particular thing or service. They were asked to be specific, and to state the specific goal(s) that they felt would be accomplished by this spending. Then they were further asked to document if that particular thing or service led to the achievement of the goals—what might be described as outcome measures. This did require more paperwork than most of the people were used to, because, you see, they had never before been asked to demonstrate the efficacy of treatments, including the $200,000-per-year residential treatment. The measurement of outcomes in Wraparound was easy and natural, however, because the focus on efficiency and the ongoing appraisal of the progress (or the lack thereof) is inherent in the approach.

As a program, AYI also made the decision to monitor its overall effectiveness and outcomes. They chose to do this by tracking the kinds of problems and behaviors that had gotten these youth in out-of-state residential treatment programs in the first place. These problems tended to be assaultive, suicidal, and/or truancy-related behaviors that had led to them to be hospitalized or placed in residential treatment and had led them to have numerous contacts with law enforcement agencies. So these are what AYI measured as outcomes. They found that there was a decrease in assaultive and suicidal behaviors, fewer contacts with the law, increased days in school, and the intensity of treatment setting decreased, with most youth ending up at home or in home-like settings. These findings were true both for an overwhelming majority of individual young people and for the program as a whole.

You may have noticed that when describing the outcomes of AYI, I used the words "decreased" and "increased" rather than suggesting that the problems went away completely. Sometimes, we set outcome goals for programs that are just unrealistic. The young people in AYI were the ones who had cost the state the most money to treat and who had the greatest number of problems. We cannot expect these particular youngsters to get completely better. While some might and do get significantly better, many of these youth should be considered to be doing well if all that happens is that they get better than they had been before. And that is what happened to almost all of them, and at the same time, the cost went down. If this is not the definition of cost-effectiveness, I don't know what is. At the end of his story, Karl worries that we are not always measuring the right things as people judge the efficacy of Wraparound. When AYI was being developed, they called on Karl and Kaleidoscope to help them develop their approach. I guess they listened to him.

As I said earlier, I started my commentary on this chapter by saying something about, "In an ideal world, cost-effectiveness would not be an issue." Karl's stories are based on the reality of the world we live in and in which we have to develop our interventions. To make our care as efficient as possible, leading to the best possible outcomes, we need to maximize the resources that we have at hand. Karl's experiences help us learn how to go about finding more services in our communities than we ever knew were there, both formal and informal. Following Karl's wisdom will help us be most effective and efficient—and will at the same time bring down the cost of intervention.

everything is NORMAL until proven otherwise

A Story About One Person's Introduction to Wraparound

I finished my psychiatric residency about the same time that Karl came to Kaleidoscope. By the time we first met in 1977, we found that we had begun to think very much alike in our approach to young people. When we met for the second time in 1985, our basic ways of thinking had become close to identical—and neither of us had even heard the term "Wraparound." Through our experiences working with youth, each of us had evolved an understanding of how to help them with their problems. The purpose of this chapter is to demonstrate that the principles and practices of what we now call Wraparound evolved over time—for both Karl and myself, from our own roots and experiences—and, hopefully, they will continue to evolve further in the future. Karl's stories demonstrate the evolution of his thought. The story of the evolution of my thought is in this chapter.

Although, of course, I feel my story is the most interesting reading in the world, that is not the reason that I feel it belongs in this book. Rather, I think it leads to an important lesson of how each of us needs to incorporate the learning of others with our own experience and develop theory and practice that works for us. In this way, you will become the future of Wraparound as you add lessons from your life and work into the meaning of Wraparound.

When I started my training in psychiatry, I was fascinated more with the struggles of adolescents in the world of adults than I was with the lessons in psychopathology that I was being taught. After all, I did this training in the first years of the 1970s, an era that culminated the youth revolution of the 1960s. During this period in history, the message from youth was that adult culture was misguided, if not corrupt, and that as a societal subculture, the only answer for youth was to become alienated from it. "Never trust a person over 30!" was a more valid motto defining this group than the more popular, "Sex, Drugs, and Rock n' Roll!" The youth mores of this era not only affected young adults, but also teenagers. As a result, oppositional behavior toward parents and intolerance of parental values became the norm, rather than an aberration. To tell your parents to get lost, or even to run away and join a street culture, was no longer necessarily seen as crazy or pathological behavior—it was just one normalized choice available to youth.

My training took place in a mental hospital that doubled as a community mental health center. We had some adolescents on our hospital wards and a program that worked with them separately from the adults during the day. (Today we are loath to place teens on wards with mentally ill adults, but in those days there was a thought that children and adults together made a more family-style atmosphere.) My teenage patients at that hospital were of two types. I had a range of teens from 14 to 18 years old as inpatients, and I had a number of older teens or young adults from 18 to 21 with whom I ran an outpatient therapy group. From these young people I learned a lot about how the care of teenagers with troubles differs dramatically from that of adults and younger children. But I also learned that they represented a very special group of adolescents and did not reflect the teenage population at large, who were getting their mental health care from other sources: drop-in centers, runaway houses, and through street workers. I would characterize these programs as "alternative youth services." (I had not yet learned that there was also a large group of teens served by school, juvenile justice programs, and social service departments.) These alternative programs grew out of the alienation between youth and traditional mental health and other services, and indeed, the leadership and staff of these programs had great disdain for more traditional services. And the youth seemed to connect with this disdain, and came to trust these new "mental health workers." The 1960s and '70s produced as many troubled youth as any era—maybe even more— but teen mores of that period lead a great number of them to mistrust all but the alternative forms of service.

I felt that if I was going to learn about caring for adolescents, I needed to get out of my mental health center and into the streets. I decided to spend an evening in a drop-in center. I tried to fit in and failed miserably. I found myself at a loss as to how to relate to these young people. Part of this reflected unresolved feelings of inadequacy from my own youth, but just as importantly, it reflected the fact that the professional stance I had learned was not applicable in this situation. I was used to sitting at my desk and having individuals, even teens, sit and talk to me about their lives. This new brand of teen was not willing to do this. They needed me to get away from my desk and my professional aloofness before they could feel comfortable relating to me, and I couldn't do it. I was willing to meet them where I was, but they needed me to meet them where they were.

This truth came to me few years later when I went to work at the National Institute of Mental Health as its Coordinator of Runaway Programs. In that position, I was able to get to know the leadership among those agencies across the country that were using alternative approaches to youth. These folks taught that the basic premise of these alternative services was captured in two mottos. The first of these was "Meeting youth where they are!" This was the same lesson that I had learned on my own, except the message from the alternative service movement was more complex. "Meeting youth where they are," had meaning at two levels. At one level, it meant just what I had already learned, that if young people were in the street one should meet them there. It also had a deeper meaning, however; it meant that we have to meet young people's mindsets. We have to understand youth culture and we have to understand what each youth's individual concerns are. We have to try and get into their heads and be there with them.

The second motto of the alternative service movement was "Changing services to meet the changing needs of youth!" I came to understand that this was also true on two different levels. The first of these levels referred to the fact that in general, the youth of the 1960s and '70s had different needs than those of the '40s and '50s, and required differently constructed services. The second level referred to the fact that for each individual teen, his or her needs were changing all the time. This meant that on any one day an individual might have a completely different set of needs than on the day before or the day after.

When I was still in training, I had not yet figured this out. I had a gut feeling that I had to do something different to meet the needs of the predominant group of youth of the day. Yet I didn't seem to fit or feel comfortable getting away from my professional posture to be able to relate to them like an alternative service worker. Not only had I failed at working at a drop-in center, I also spent a few days at a group-home drug program in the role of a teen client, because the staff felt they could only relate to me as a psychiatrist if I really knew what it was like to be in the shoes of one of their clients. I'm not sure if they were right, but I passed their test and they allowed me to work with them as a consultant. One of the things I learned through that particular experience was that I couldn't loosen up enough to work with youth in that type of intensive, down-and-dirty environment—even though I could consult as a psychiatrist. On one level, I saw this as another failure in my adaptation to the new mental health for youth, but on another level, a strange thing happened to me as a result of that experience: I began to change.

I had been running a psychotherapy group of older teens and young adults, folks from the ages of 18 to 22 or so. This was at a community mental health center, which in reality was an old, urban, state mental hospital. Some of the older rooms and offices had huge bulky 19th-century keys. The room in which the group was held required one of these old keys. I would show up a minute or so before the group with my cotherapist, open the door with my big key, and invite the group to join us. When the group ended, my cotherapist and I would leave last, shut the door with the big key and go our separate ways. A few weeks after my unsuccessful foray into the drop-in center, however, I found myself sitting on the front steps of the hospital about a half-hour before the time for the group with its members sitting around me. We weren't discussing problems or deep personal issues, we were talking about the rock concert that was to be held in a city park that night. Then, of course, when the group time came, we got up and went to the room, which I opened with the big key, and when the group was over I closed the door with my big key and went on my way.

I tell you this story because I see it as a turning point in my mental health career. On the surface, the change was not a great one. I merely spent a short time with my group as a friend before changing back into the therapist I had always been. But to me, and maybe even the group, the change was profound. While I couldn't work in a drop-in center or a drug program as a youth worker, I could find my own personal solution to doing a better job of meeting youth where they were. I had begun to give up the traditional approach in which I was being trained so that I could do what I thought was a better, more relevant job. In retrospect, even though sitting outside the hospital with my group was not a planned or even conscious decision—by that time I had come to the conclusion that I couldn't change—in retrospect, with that simple move I began my career in Wraparound.

I learned that when a teenager did something that looked weird or crazy, I should not make a judgment about that young person based on that behavior alone. Instead, I learned to ask about what that particular behavior meant. For example (as I mentioned earlier), was a runaway episode a good runaway or a problematic one? By that I meant, did the kid end up in a safe house or commune, or did he or she end up prostituting him or herself on the street? The act of running away itself did not define who the child was. One had to take all kinds of factors into consideration to do that.

One of those factors was the normal developmental process of childhood. In my training, I was learning that adolescence is a particularly difficult time in development. During this period of a person's life he or she must make the shift from being a child to being an adult. For this to happen certain important transitions must take place. The first of these, which many people think is the most important, is the process of separation from one's family. This means giving up the dependency that we have on our families and learning to be a separate individual. To allow this to happen, young people must learn to be part of a peer group and begin to rely on peer relationships in meeting some of their dependency needs. At the same time they have to make the transition from school to work (for many of us, college put off this task for several years). Bodies grow very rapidly during this stage of life, and teens mature sexually and physically. Every adolescent must struggle with and adapt to these and other changes. At the same time, every parent and guardian must make similar adaptations.

Some people refer to the teen years as being a "crazy" period, during which families and children must learn to adjust to each other's changes. Ongoing debate exists among professionals as to just how crazy a period adolescence is. I have accepted the position that some adolescents have a lot of craziness in their lives and still should be considered normal, while other adolescents handle the developmental changes of their stage in life without much disruption of their lives being apparent to others. Still other adolescents, who bring individual and/or family problems into adolescence, find that this stage in life exaggerates those problems and makes them more difficult to deal with than they were earlier in life. And for others still, adolescence is an era in which major mental illness emerges.

I have come to the conclusion that when something crazy happens with an adolescent, it is very difficult to tell if that particular craziness is part of a normal child's struggle with this difficult stage of life, or if the crazy-looking behavior or thought is really the expression of some significant emotional problem or mental illness. Am I looking at a mood, a bad day, a temporary problem (i.e., a developmental struggle), or a long-term illness? The problem is that each of these can look exactly the same in terms of a child's behavior or thinking. I chose to base my initial response to a youth's troubled behavior on the premise that that particular behavior was normal. Was I always right? Of course not. But by making a normal interpretation of the behavior, I gave the youth a chance to be normal. This was very different than what I was learning in my formal training. There, I was being taught to take the behavior as I viewed it, put it together with other behaviors that other adults had viewed, and ultimately to regard those behaviors as "symptoms" that define some diagnosis of psychopathology or mental illness. The problem with doing this, however, was that even if the behavior was part of a normal pattern in a particular youngster, or if the behavior was just the result of a bad day or even a bad week or month, I would end up giving that youth a diagnosis.

A diagnosis is very hard to get rid of after you receive it. You get labeled as what the diagnosis is. However much that labeling and stigma is a problem, an even greater problem is that as soon as you are given a diagnosis, someone begins to treat you on the basis of that diagnosis. In the late 1960s and early '70s that didn't make a lot sense. Most adolescents looked crazy and did things that looked crazy to adults, but most didn't have a psychopathology or mental illness that needed to be treated. Most of them just needed understanding and support. In the hospital where I trained, we treated them like "mental patients." Those same youth when they went to the new alternative youth services were treated like "children." Where do you think they did better? This taught me to accept the behaviors and issues of youth as expressions of where they were only at that particular moment and to give them credit for having more to them than they were showing me that day. They reciprocated by showing their best when they had the chance.

This was my first lesson in having a strength-based approach. I didn't understand it that way then. I had another explanation. I came up with what I called Lourie's First Law of Adolescence: *Everything is normal until proven otherwise*. Today, some 25 years later, this is still the message I give myself every morning. There's an old joke about the sea captain of great renown who every morning opened his safe and read from a sheet of paper. He would never tell anyone what was on the paper and would never let anyone look over his shoulder to read it. Those around him were sure it was the secret of his success and were anxious to learn the great lessons that the captain had on this sheet. When the old captain died, the first thing his followers did, of course, was open the safe to learn the great secret. When they looked, they were dumbfounded. What the paper said was merely, "Port is on the left and starboard is on the right!" These of course were among the simplest of nautical rules, but often hard for many people to remember. Lourie's First Law is also a very simple message, but, given the reaction of most folks to adolescent behaviors and the professional push toward pathologizing behaviors that are seen as different, it is a hard message to adhere to. So every morning, all of us should open our safes and read the simple but important message: everything is normal until proven otherwise.

For me, the other principles of Wraparound naturally flowed from this premise (with the exception of the family strengths focus, which unfortunately took me much more time to learn). As soon as I convinced youth that I would not judge them on the basis of their momentary crazinesses, they began to teach me other things. They taught me that they lived in communities and families and that is where they should continue to live as long as possible. They taught me to appreciate their individual differences, especially those that derived from living in different cultures. They also taught me that they expect those who really care for them will not give up on them easily, or will not give up on them at all. They need adults who will be there for them through some tough times, including some times when they push you away (which, of course, is developmentally appropriate for individuals of that age as part of the normal adolescent separation process). All of these things, of course, became my own personal version of the major principles of Wraparound.

By the time Karl and I met, each of us had developed our own understanding of how to approach youth who have problems. My view was expressed through the saying "Everything is normal until proven otherwise." Karl's view was expressed through his focus on the principles of unconditional care and a strength-based approach. We found our views to be extremely compatible—maybe even the same—and ten years later, we found them to be called *Wraparound*. The lesson I would like the reader to take away from my story is that each of us needs to understand children, adolescents, and their families in their own unique way, and then try and find the ways in which those ideas fit with Karl's, mine, and the principles of Wraparound. In that way, Wraparound will continue to evolve as both people and society change.

the first family I provided care to

Stories about Karl's Philosophy and the
Evolution of Wraparound

I'll always remember the first family to whom I provided care. I was lucky enough to be asked to provide care to a family and I used the techniques that I had been taught. The first thing I did was to sit down and read all the material available about them. As I look back today, it is amazing how much of that material was negative. But at that time in my career, it did not bother me, and after reading the material, I figured out what this family needed and started to put a plan together for them. Only then did I go out to visit them. I remember talking to the mom, whose name was Agnes. I told her how happy I was to see her and that I could be of some help with providing some services to her. She told me how happy she was for me to be there. I told her about the plan I had developed. I explained that with this plan we would share; I would do some of the things on the plan and she would do some of the things on the plan. She seemed pleased, and I left feeling very confident that the plan would work.

After a week it became very clear that I had done all the things on my list and Agnes hadn't done any on hers. I assumed it was because she was busy, so I did some of her things. This happened the second week, the third week, and by the fifth week strange things started creeping into my paperwork—phrases like, "Not amenable to treatment!" and other similar language we like to use when people are resistant to the decisions we make for them.

As I continued to see her, I was getting pretty frustrated, but she was still saying she was willing to do her things on the list. Then during one visit, I noticed there was a mirror behind Agnes, which allowed me to see that although she was talking to me with a smile on her face, behind her back she had her middle finger pointed at the ceiling. It rapidly became clear to me that what she really wanted to say to me was that I could go to hell!

In that moment, the earliest concepts of what we now call Wraparound services began to form in my mind. Although my first reaction to Agnes giving me "the finger" could have been for me to give it back to her—by continuing to say, "Not amenable to treatment!"—I fortunately took another direction. I realized that she had finally given me the answer to why the plan wasn't working. She was teaching me that the real key here was not for me to create the plan by myself. Rather, I needed to sit down with her so that we could become creative together and formulate a plan together. That way, not only would we develop a plan that she was in favor of, but more importantly, it would be a plan that she was in charge of. After Agnes and I did that, the plan worked!

This was my first lesson in learning how to give up the old approach in which I had been taught to plan for other people based only on my professional knowledge and opinions. I found out that it was better to sit down with people and plan with them around whatever they felt was important and needed. I learned about the positive power families have within them, even when things aren't working well for them. This is a prime element of Wraparound.

In the rest of this chapter, I will discuss all the major elements of Wraparound. I'm going to do it in a different way than in the earlier parts of this book, however. Most of this book is structured around what had been designated as the ten elements of Wraparound in the early 1990s by a group of people from around the country who had been instrumental in the development of Wraparound as a an intervention. This group was called the International Initiative on the Development, Training, and Evaluation of Wraparound Services. When that group came together in 1991 and 1992, we agreed on a single language to use to describe Wraparound. These elements are summarized in Chapter 2 about Cindy, and are the basis around which I organize my teaching and most of my lectures.

Wraparound did not get created this way, however. In the first chapter of this book, I tell of how Kaleidoscope and I came to develop No Reject, No Eject, Unconditional Care Services. In the chapter before this one, Ira tells of how he came to the same conclusions about how people needed to be offered services, although he took a much different path than mine. And, while our conclusions were the essentially the same, we each had our own way of talking about it. Others in the field each had their own ways of coming to similar conclusions. In this chapter, I hope to impress upon you that there are many ways of conceptualizing Wraparound, but no matter how one states it, it is essentially the same. I am going to tell you about some of the experiences I've had in my professional life that have been memorable to me in my understanding of Wraparound. While they roughly relate to the "elements of Wraparound" that I still use, they are not an exact translation. This is all right, because in the long run, all of the elements run together and could be cut up in any number of ways to compile a formal "list of elements."

Agnes taught me about the strength of families, the need for flexibility, the need for participation and sharing, the need for team decisionmaking, and the need to give up my professional power to families. A 9-year-old named Rodney, who had been in residential placement and hospitals for the last three years of his life before coming to Kaleidoscope, also taught me a few things. One night, after he had been in Kaleidoscope's services for a while, I took Rodney to dinner. As we finished dinner he asked me a question that I didn't immediately understand. "Are you paying for this dinner?"

My first thought was, "Of course I'm paying for this dinner!" Then I realized he knew that and what he was really asking was another question: "Are *you* paying for this dinner or is your agency paying for this dinner?"

It occurred to me that all Rodney wanted to know was if I cared enough about him to pay for this dinner personally or was it like what he had seen in the past, where people were nice to him only because it was part of their job and the cost of dinner came out of institutional dollars. He was simply asking the question, "Do you care about me?" It really moved me, and I was happy to report to him that in this particular case it was coming out of my pocket.

There was a greater lesson to be learned from this experience with Rodney about how important it is for the people to whom we provide care to see what our commitment is. I've always suggested that our commitment to the people we serve should be the same as the one we have to our own families. Now while on some occasions I have wanted to, I cannot conceive giving up on my own children. Therefore, I feel that I should not give up on anyone else's child. Once you have said to someone that you're going to be there for them no matter what, you had better be there! Otherwise, you become just another one of the people who have let them down, often as they have moved from placement to placement. Your own children and the children you serve both deserve an unconditional commitment. The parents who are reading this chapter know this, but the service people need to understand that only with unconditional care will the children and families who rely on you feel comfortable enough to grow under your care. This was not the first lesson I ever learned about the Wraparound element of unconditional care, but

Rodney's question was a powerful reminder to me of just how important it is. We all need a reminder now and then.

To provide unconditional care, one has to do lots of things. You have to be flexible enough to frequently change the services you are providing to a child and family. This ensures that you are continually doing what is necessary to meet their needs at any particular point in time. There is no way you can do this in the structure of an inflexible program. Instead, Wraparound has to be a process that focuses on people's individual strengths and needs, their own unique background, family and culture, and the community they live in. The next stories tell about what it takes to do Wraparound.

One of the most important things I learned about providing services was supplied to me by Cindy, who you read about in the beginning of this book. As you may remember, in that chapter Ira wrote about how Cindy was the teacher who taught me a tremendous amount about all of the elements of Wraparound. In my own words, the major lesson she taught me was that no matter how poorly people feel about their own situation, their own children, or their station in life (Cindy was a prostitute and the system said that she didn't care about her child), there is always something in every person that has a fire and a spark. This comes from their strengths. Cindy taught me that if you can touch those strengths and partner with them, you will see growth. In Cindy's case, it was not so much her growth alone; it was also the growth of all of the people around her, including the Kaleidoscope staff. Cindy was the fire that fed herself and the people around her, and all we at Kaleidoscope had to do was to help her harness that fire and let her strengths carry her forward.

Ira once asked me, "What if Cindy had refused to take a bath?" I told him that we would still have continued to provide services, but we would've made sure the apartment we moved her into had a decent shower or bathtub and we would have made sure there was soap and deodorant and those kind of things. We would've started talking about the "either/ors": for example, "Certainly, you have a right not to take a shower if you don't want to, but you need to understand that if you're going to find a job or stay in an apartment, your hygiene will be one of the things people look at. So that is something you need to think about." It's not about judging people, it's about supporting them to do better.

In addition, if she wouldn't take a bath or a shower, my thing would be use a lot of humor, a tactic that has always worked for me. I don't have a problem saying to someone, "Oooh my, you need to do something about that." As I said to Cindy when she offered me sexual favors, "Cindy, this is something that we can't even talk about until you've had a bath and gotten some teeth in your mouth." People often ask me how I get away with making jokes about serious things, and I have to admit that I'm not sure. I think it is because people are aware that I really care about them. The joke is between them and me. I think that's the key. Caring makes a big difference. I wonder if I would have appreciated the lessons I learned from Cindy as much if she had not bathed. I'd like to believe I would have found other ways to discover her strengths, but I don't know.

There are times when it's really hard to find peoples' strengths. Then it becomes a challenge, because I know the strengths are there, but sometimes you really have to stretch to find them. In my entire career I've only seen two people who I thought might not be redeemable. One of those was a person who had prostituted his wife, sexually abused his own children, gone to the penitentiary, and if that wasn't enough, was an extremely intimidating person. As a matter of fact, he once slapped the State's Attorney right in front of the judge in the courtroom. He was not too bright, but most of all, he just didn't care.

I wanted to teach him, so I gave him my line: "You can intimidate people while you are with them, but if they can get away from you, it doesn't last."

He replied, "I went home once and asked my sister and mother for some money and they refused to give it to me, so I beat them both up. Then the next time I got out of jail and I asked them for money for food and stuff, they gave it to me!" His position was that intimidation did indeed work extremely well for him. I considered him, as I suggested, to be an unredeemable person.

On the other hand, one day he said to me, "I'm not such a bad guy. I don't have my wife prostituting anymore." A lot of people might say, "So what?" But if you are looking for strengths you might say, "Hey, there's a glimmer of understanding here." Another thing you might say about him is that he's not so dumb. After all, he did figure out that intimidation is a strategy that works for him and is the direction to go in. Those are strengths that could be used with him.

I'm not sure if I can remember if there is anyone I've ever met and spent any time with who didn't have some strength. This includes the other guy I felt was unredeemable. This guy tried to beat me up, and the police had to save me from him. Yet, I did become aware of how much he cared about his children and how much he wanted to try to keep his children out of the service system. Whether he was rational or not on the day he came after me, he still had that caring inside of him.

When you discover those hidden strengths, you can work with them. They are not always obvious or easy to work with, but they are there. In fact, sometimes you need to work with a degree of faith that the strengths are there even though they might not be totally evident. It is our job to find them. I always assume that everyone I work with has strengths, and if I can't see them, I take finding them as my responsibility. It's my failure if I've been unable to find them. So that means I have to double my efforts until I do.

Sometimes there are things about people that make it difficult for another individual to find their strengths. I assume that it has something to do with the person who is looking rather than with the person being looked at; because some other person may find it easy to deal with those same things. For example, I've never had problems working with people who are considered to be really difficult, but some people just can't work with such individuals. On the other hand, I have problems working with people with alcoholism. When they are sober, I don't have problems with them, but when they are drunk, I do not do as well. That is my shortcoming, and I am aware of it and understand it. Therefore, I've always made sure I was paired with people who can work with alcoholics. With Cindy, if I couldn't have personally gotten past her hygiene, we would have found someone to work with her who could.

In addition to finding strengths in the people who come to us for help, we need to look for strengths in those people who come together to help them. This applies to the development and functioning of Child and Family Teams, one of the basic elements of Wraparound. When we work with Child and Family Teams, the facilitator of that process must look at all of the people around the table and ask one question, "What are the things each person does extremely well? What are their positives?" We always talk about listing strengths of the children and the families, but we must also discover how to utilize the strengths of all the people around the table as part of the team process. The other team members react just like the families. If you talk to them about their positives and strengths, they will be more invested in the team process. For example, giving a child protection worker credit for his or her ability to assess risk and protect children will help that person be a better and more productive team member. Finding strengths in people is one of the most basic keys of why Wraparound works.

Making our services individually oriented, community-based and culturally competent are all important aspects of Wraparound, as the next story shows. We got a call one night from Jessie, a young lady who we were serving in Kaleidoscope's Independent-Living Environment. She reported, "I'm at the police station."

A staff member replied, "I'll be right over."

"No, no, you don't have to come," She said, "It's not about me. It's about something else. They just want to interview me and I'll be able to go home. You can come by tomorrow morning and we'll talk about it."

The next morning staff went by. What they discovered was that, although they had always cautioned her about giving others access to her apartment, Jessie had allowed some friends to use it. They were a sister and brother who lived down the block from her. These two lived with their mom, and they had an argument with her, which, I was led to believe, ended with them killing her. Because they didn't know what to do with her body, they put it in a shopping cart and carried it into Jessie's apartment and left it in the closet. When Jessie came home and opened the closet, she found the dead body and reacted very reasonably—by calling the police and calling us.

Well, we were all really upset. We wanted to know where we could move her. We asked her where she would like to move, because we thought that we certainly needed to get her out of that environment.

She thought about it for a while and said, "You know, there is an apartment upstairs in the building, and I just want to move up there. As a matter of fact, I wouldn't mind staying in this apartment, except I don't think I can get the blood out of the rug."

What the staff didn't understand was that Jessie lived in the kind of community that would allow a person to think in those terms. Some people in our society have seen so much violence they don't get as freaked out about it as the rest of us. The staff did not understand where Jessie came from both individually and from the point of view of her community. They were totally freaked out and the only solution they saw to the problem at hand was a move to the other side of town. That was *their* individual and community understanding. Jessie, however, came from a community that reacted to violence in a very different way. Not that violence was acceptable, but rather it was a fact of life that the community's members had to deal with, rather than running away from it. Similarly, they did not see Jessie as an individual who needed her own personal approach to this problem she faced: one based on her individual personality and cultural values. Obviously, the staff had trained Jessie well and she didn't react to their discomfort; rather, she gave them the proper answer—for her. Jessie knew her community; she felt comfortable and had supports there. Another important aspect of the staff's response to Jessie's predicament is that, before condemning her for the behavior that got her into this predicament in the first place, the staff needed to find out if sharing her apartment with friends was a part of her cultural upbringing and a strength to be honed rather than a fault to be eradicated. Jessie taught me how important it is to understand what people's unique qualities are: what they are like as individuals, how they react to things, what help they need, how they fit into and relate to their community, how their own special cultural values must be part of how we offer them service, and, of course, what their individual strengths are. All these things are pieces of the elements of Wraparound.

Being individualized in our approach to helping people meet their needs requires us to be flexible and creative. I think we did this with a young man and his family for whom we were planning during a Wraparound training session. As usual, during this planning exercise, we asked the people who organized the training to bring in a family and their child for whom they were having difficulty planning. The family they brought in consisted of a young man and his parents. Tad had been suspended from school for cursing. Even though he was a young person who had a number of issues in school, they were focused on the cursing and said he was going to be suspended indefinitely if he cursed again. Whether or not his cursing was clinically based or not did not seem to be the issue to me. The issue seemed to be, how could we keep Tad in school? When we asked him if he thought he could stop cursing, Tad suggested that he didn't think he could get that done. As we talked with his family we discovered that Tad's grandfather, who lived nearby, had been born in Poland. So, we put two and two together and came up with a suggestion; we would ask the grandfather to teach the young man how to curse in Polish. In this way, anytime he felt he couldn't restrain himself from cursing, he would do so in Polish. Since nobody would know what he was saying, he would get the opportunity to stay in school. We thought that the folks who worked with Tad and his family would have the time later to find other ways to work on stopping him from cursing altogether, but at this particular point we had an intervention for solving the crisis as it existed at the moment; and, it worked to keep Tad in school.

Sometimes when we come up with a creative and individualized solution to a problem, we like to try to use it with other young people; after all, not all interventions have to be different. Once while doing another training, we were asked after our meeting to come and have a conversation with a young lady, Becky, who had been hospitalized numerous times. Her mom had been very active in working with and for Becky. This seemed to have worked extremely well, yet Mom was still pretty much at her wits' end. Becky had spent over 200 days in the hospital for physical issues, was unhappy in life, and did not know how long she was going to live.

So we went talk to her. The first thing she said to us was that she didn't really want to be bothered and turned her back. All attempts to involve her were failing. Since nothing else had worked, I tried an intervention with Becky that I usually do with boys. In this intervention, I look at the persons' room for the purpose of finding out something about them. I look at what they've put up on their walls, which helps me see what moves them and what's important to them. So, I asked her, "May I see your room?"

Becky grunted, "Why would you want to do that?"

Not to be put off by a grunt, I told her, "A lot of times, I can learn things about people that way." And continued gingerly, "Would you mind?"

She softened a bit and said that she wouldn't mind. Well, the first thing I noticed was that for a 13-year-old, her room was immaculate. Everything was neat, and on one shelf she had maybe 20 different dolls, which were all lined up.

I asked her, "Do you like dolls?"

She said, "Yes, I love dolls."

Having gotten a conversation started, I took a gamble and asked, "May I ask you, why don't you want to talk to us?"

"Because you professionals don't know how to treat kids," she replied.

"Oh," I said, "You know, we once asked a parent to give us a list of dos and don'ts for working with parents, and that helped us learn how to treat parents better. Would you be willing to do a list of dos and don'ts for working with kids for us? If you agree, I'll buy you a doll to add to your collection."

She agreed to do it.

I told her, "You can mail us the list when you get it done."

She said, "I don't have to. I can e-mail it to you!" She had just let us know that she was pretty fluent on the computer.

By that time, she was willing to have a conversation with us, and we were able to suggest that we had a friend with the same physical ailment she had, who was still alive and kicking in his 40s or 50s. We asked, "Would you like to have him as a contact person so that you can have someone who has lived with your illness to talk to about it with?"

Again, she agreed.

This got us down to the last issue, which was her cursing. She wasn't cursing so much at school, but she was cursing in the house, and her mom had a difficult time tolerating it. Well, I thought about the cursing intervention we had done for Tad and it turned out that our oldest daughter was just back from Kenya, and was fluent in Swahili. I asked Becky, "If we could teach you to curse in Swahili, would you substitute that for cursing in English?"

Again, she agreed.

Unfortunately, a problem came when we discovered, upon talking to our daughter, that there are really no curse words in Swahili. So much for repeated interventions. But, what did help Becky was the fact we were willing to see her as an individual with a unique set of problems and to work with her as she was. Interventions don't always turn out the way you want them to, but what made a difference with Becky was that we made a special effort geared just to her, and so she was willing to try some different things and some new ways of running her life. She did send us a list and she did get her doll.

All of us can still be more individualized in our approach to children and their families, whether or not we work in a Wraparound or a traditional, categorical agency. I never really understood why that simple concept is so difficult for people to accept. We do it all the time in our own personal lives. If you have two good friends, for example, you may be able to tell one of them to go to hell and get away without it being a problem—it just may be the way the two of you are comfortable communicating. At the same time, your other friend might be offended by similar language or thought. You would probably already know this, so with that friend you would take another approach to disagreeing with him or her. It is the same with our own families. We always individualize when we approach the people we have contact with day in and day out. Why wouldn't we do the same thing with the people we provide services to? Not only does it make logical sense, it makes for good Wraparound.

When I talked about Agnes at the beginning of this chapter, I focused on how she had changed the way I understood the role families need to take in developing and participating in their own care or the care of their children, and how we have to give parents credit for knowing what they need in order to help their children. Now I want to tell you about some other important things I've learned from families. One of those families lived in one of the most notorious housing projects in the City of Chicago. There was a mom, Patricia, who had three children, 11, 12, and 5 years old. The 5-year-old, Richard, was one of those children who needed a lot of help from the service system in Chicago. Unfortunately, he wasn't quite needy enough. For example, if there were six criteria for obtaining a service, Richard always would only have met five. As a result, Patricia found the services she could, but for the most part wound up taking over Richard's care herself—while at the same time trying to hold down a job so she and her family could live. One of the problems Richard had was that he never slept, and eventually Patricia suffered from sleep deprivation. In addition, he had torn holes in the couch and broken out windows, all of which had traumatized her two older children. Patricia ran out of energy and stopped being able to give her children all the care they needed, and so one day they showed up at school dirty. The school reported this to child protective services. A caseworker who was sent to Richard's home in the projects came to the conclusion that "this woman" was "dysfunctional" and that her children needed to be taken away from her because she "just doesn't have the parenting skills to take care of them."

Another family who lived in one of our more wealthy suburbs around Chicago had a similar experience. The mom in this family, Janice, also had a number of children, but she was more fortunate in that she was financially stable. When she began seeing the problems her son, Jimmy, had, she immediately got in touch with her physician. He put her in touch with a good psychiatrist who had Jimmy hospitalized. And then, one of the miracles of western civilization occurred. The very day that Jimmy ran out of insurance coverage he was determined to be cured! He returned home, but Janice's insurance would not pay for any additional services. So she paid out of her pocket for as much service as she could afford. This included one year in which she paid $30,000 for Jimmy's services! Eventually, she ran out of money. She had to sell her house, take her children out of private school, and move into an apartment, while at the same time continuing to look for services for Jimmy. As with Patricia, she wasn't getting the help or support she needed to take care of her son, so she got overwhelmed and her other children began having problems in school. This school, too, reported the family to protective services, which sent a social worker to her home who suggested that "this woman" was "dysfunctional" and was a bad parent. Again the decision was for her children to be taken away from her...and they were.

What these stories and many other similar ones have taught me is that there are very few dysfunctional families in this country. Rather, there are a lot of dysfunctional systems that simply don't provide services that are appropriate or timely enough to offer the Patricias and Janices the help they need to care for their children. And, when the systems we have in place to help families fail, we blame the families and call them "dysfunctional." The lesson I learned from this is that we need to be very careful not to label people we don't know as "dysfunctional" based on what other people have written about them. When we meet people, we need to take the opportunity to sit down with them and learn the truth and the reality of their situation, their history, and environmental circumstances. Only then would I pass any type of judgment on them. By that time, I would have learned more about how functional they are and have been.

I have become convinced that the difference between me and the people for whom I provide services is simply a matter of circumstances. For example, at one time Kaleidoscope created a basketball team with some youth who were receiving our services and some youth who were children of staff members; on this team you couldn't tell which young people were which. In keeping with that, I felt it was important to include my family in the lives and activities of the families we serve.

My own children grew up participating socially and otherwise with youth and families being served by Kaleidoscope. There was a time when one of the Kaleidoscope youth came to me to report that my son was dating one of the young ladies in our independent living services. My response was to ask the reporting youth, "What's the big deal? Are you any different because you get services from Kaleidoscope?" In the first chapter of the book, we wrote about how we at Kaleidoscope put our independent living apartments near college campuses, as I said, because "no matter how bizarre our youth were, if we placed them around universities, they wouldn't look any more bizarre than the freshman class at that university."

Another instance concerned my daughter and one of the young ladies being served by Kaleidoscope. This woman was considered to be one of the most dangerous people in the Illinois system and she had already had two children taken away from her. Well, this person made friends with my daughter not long after my daughter gave birth to my grandson. It was very interesting to see how my daughter took a different approach to this young woman than the system had; she allowed her to play with my grandson and to spend time with him. Not only did this experience seem to be very helpful for her, it was also a growth experience for my daughter. If we truly believe in the strengths of those we serve, one of the most powerful ways we can demonstrate it is to be willing ourselves and through our families to practice what we preach.

Now that we've discussed some of the basic things that go into Wraparound, like being unconditional, letting families have ownership of the process, focusing on strengths, being truly individualized and culturally competent, being creative and flexible in developing and delivering service options, and seeing family members as people like ourselves, let us discuss what has to happen in order to get Wraparound done. I'm not going to talk about how to put together a Child and Family Team, or create an interagency collaboration team to make Wraparound work—we've discussed these issues in depth in earlier chapters. Rather, I'm going to tell about the ways of looking at service delivery that makes Wraparound different than the "same-old, same-old" that other service providers and system agencies offer.

When we think about Wraparound, it is imperative to understand that it is not a program. A program suggests something that has specific interventions and approaches. Instead, Wraparound should be viewed as a process. A process suggests something fluid with ever-changing interventions and approaches as need be. In order to make sure we don't fall into "program thinking" within Wraparound, I always talk in terms of environments as opposed to programs. The reason I do this is very simple; I think the term "environment" suggests a place where a person lives while receiving any one of many services that they require. When we talk about putting a person in a "program," it suggests we've already determined what type of services they will receive, and once they are there they can only receive the services that the program offers. For example, you might feel a certain child may be in need of a level-system form of behavior management. If you think only in terms of "program," you would look at all the programs you could find with level systems and figure out which one the child best fits into and then place him or her there—if that program had a vacancy. The catch is the wording "the child best fits into." This defines a compromise between a best fit and a perfect fit, kind of like the "square peg in the round hole" thing. On the other hand, when you think in terms of "environments," you look for the best environment for the child (which could be at home), and then you fit a level system around the child in that environment. The catch wording here is, "fit...around the child." Now, we have a jigsaw-puzzle kind of thing with "a unique shaped peg in a hole with a perfect fit"! This defines the Wraparound process.

Another aspect of Wraparound that makes it special is that there are certain skills I think people need to have in order to make it work, and they're not the kind of skills usually considered in professional circles. The first thing is that you have to be able to relinquish control. Most people who have worked to help others do so from the following point of view: "I have been trained to know what you need, therefore I'm the boss and it is my job to dictate to you what you need to do!"—much as I first approached Agnes. To give up this attitude is an intensely difficult thing, and as we have watched Wraparound grow, this has been the thing that has most baffled people. Much of this is related to how we are educated. People just coming out of an undergraduate or graduate school program will have little, if any, training about community services and community systems. They do not get to learn about unconditional care, strengths, interagency collaboration, and family participation. For the most part, they are taught to work in one or two program settings. On the contrary, to do a Wraparound process, you need to unlearn many of the program-oriented lessons you were taught, and learn how to let the family and their helpers work together as a team to get things done and help things get better.

To do Wraparound, most people have to change the way they have been trained to do things, and this is not so easy. It is similar to my first father-in-law's struggle with a young man who was his neighbor. My father-in-law was deacon of a church. His young neighbor had became a leader in the Black Panthers and had an Afro hairstyle. At that time the Afro was a sign of Black Power, and he was one of the first people to wear one. Now, my father-in-law had been raised to believe that one needed to look and act as White as you possibly could. To achieve this, he did things like wearing a stocking cap on his head at night to straighten his hair. Then suddenly, with his Afro, his neighbor is saying to him, "No, you shouldn't do that! You need to be proud you are Black!" So they fought about this. This makes sense, because if my father-in-law had accepted what this young man was saying as correct, he would have had to admit that he had been wrong all those years—a hard, if not impossible, hurdle for him to get across. What I suggest to people about service delivery is not that they've been doing things wrong; it's just that there is something new. It's a growth process, and Wraparound is another thing you can add to your bag of tricks in working with families.

Something else people have to change in order to do Wraparound is to give up being in charge. Rather than being a boss, you need to be a salesperson, and this is just what some of the best people who do Wraparound work are. To be a salesperson you need to have a personality that allows you to become friends with people, or at least to give that impression. You need to be a self-starter, to be able to get up and get out, because nobody's going to be looking over your shoulder when you're working with families and are out in the community. Most importantly, you need to be able to look past the issues people have brought to you and sell them on the power of their own strengths. This is something we have to keep doing over and over again with families and sometimes other Child and Family Team members.

In traditional services, control of the treatment process is a major issue, with professionals making it clear that they are the ones running things. In Wraparound we try to give the family as much control as possible, so we call the person who organizes the Child and Family Team and its intervention a "facilitator." Unlike in other forms of intervention, the "facilitator" of a Wraparound Child and Family Team is not necessarily a professional. It could be a parent, an aunt or uncle, a professional, or anyone who is part of the team. It is important to understand that the facilitator's role does not include control; rather it focuses on making sure control does not become an issue. The facilitator is not the team leader! There is no designated leader because as soon as you start to designate leaders, control becomes an issue. It's always difficult for people, whether they're families or professionals, not only relinquish control but to relinquish some of their own opinions about how things need to go. The facilitator's job is to help the team members do just this.

People who do Wraparound also need to be willing to take some risk. One day a colleague of mine, John VanDenBerg, said to me, "Hey, Karl, what are you going to do when you get fired?"

"What do you mean, when I get fired?," I replied.

He said, "Don't you think that you're going to get fired if you keep doing this kind of work?"

John said this to me in 1985, just as he was starting to work on the first big state Wraparound program, the Alaska Youth Initiative, which was based on Kaleidoscope's Wraparound process. John told me that he kept a wood plane in his office, because he used to be a carpenter and he knew that if he got fired he could always go back to being a carpenter.

My response to John was, "Well, when I got this job I was looking for a job, so if I get fired, I won't be worse off than the day that I got hired."

We both laughed about it, but we knew that if you try to help people by supporting their strengths rather than focusing entirely on their weaknesses, there are times that the weaknesses will win out over the strengths and bad things happen. When bad things happen in programs, somehow working for the program protects you. In Wraparound, you are a bit more vulnerable when these bad things happen. In my mind, the key to reducing risk is trying to figure out for yourself what the positive and right thing to do is. One of the things that has always worked for me is to ask myself a simple question, "What would I have done for my family in a similar circumstance?" I also think it is important to make team decisions. This way each individual on the team is protected by the team decisionmaking process. You can minimize risk by keeping solutions simple and following up. We keep risk down when we remember that Wraparound is simply a matter of finding families, asking what they need, providing them with what they need, and never, ever giving up. That is how we at Kaleidoscope saw the Wraparound process, and it is basically what makes it work.

Sometimes people say Wraparound is difficult and everybody who does it needs to be exceptional. I believe that not everyone needs to be the best. This is because the Wraparound process inspires people who work with it, both professionals and family members, to rise above the place where they have always been. In traditional program-based services, I think it is easy to get discouraged. At the point when things get rough, these programs tend to give up on the children and reject them. When this happens, all of the energy the workers have put into that child is lost, or worse, turned against the child and his or her family. When things do work, it is sometimes three, four, or five years down the line before we see the results. With Wraparound, however, when you put a plan together, you will most often start to see something happen instantly, especially in terms of the support and help people feel. When things don't work, in Wraparound, we don't bail out on the child and family, rather we work together as a team to come up with new solutions. These things help all of the people involved do their best and keep getting better at what they do.

As we come to the end of this book, it is important for Ira and I to reiterate one major point: Wraparound is not a program, rather it is a philosophy and a way of approaching things. How one "does" Wraparound is constantly changing. First, it changes for each individual based on that individual's strengths and those of his or her family. Secondly, the concepts of Wraparound change over time as we who do Wraparound figure it out better. You see, Wraparound is still evolving as an approach.

Ira was once visiting Kaleidoscope, and was leafing through the agency training manuals, when he turned to me and remarked, "You know, I can't find the word 'Wraparound' in here."

I responded, "Ira, when we first started doing this, nobody called it 'Wraparound'. It was just 'What we do at Kaleidoscope'. Our training manual predates us calling this 'Wraparound' and there has been no need to change it. The other part is that I really have tried to be extremely careful about keeping things flexible. One of the things that has made this whole process kind of difficult for me is that I don't want things etched in stone.

"More and more Wraparound is becoming prescribed. People are saying, 'You have to do this, or you have to do that, to do Wraparound.' My thing is, if you follow the basic elements, you should wind up doing good Wraparound. If what we do becomes extremely structured, it will lose its creativity and won't be very individualized. When you focus only on the structure of a Wraparound process, you can do all the 'right' things and still come up with a bad plan if you haven't included those basic elements of the philosophy in the process. If you stick with the basic elements of Wraparound, over the long run there is never a bad plan, because the plan changes all the time. If you develop a plan that does not work, obviously it's not a good plan, and therefore you need to redo it. You keep redoing it until things get better. And if you stick with it, they will."

Then Ira, who is always thinking, said, "It's a good thing we have this on tape—it would be a great way to end the book!"

While this may be the end of the book, this is not the final word on Wraparound. The Wraparound concept is still evolving. Over the years since individualized service approaches were first started at Kaleidoscope and other agencies, some of those approaches have come to be called "Wraparound." As we have said before, in the early 1990s a consensus group came together and produced some elements that we all felt were the basis of Wraparound. These are the ten elements we talk about in this book. Since that time, while I have stuck with the elements as they were described in 1992, others have modified them in concert with their own growing experience in doing Wraparound. In 1998, the federal Center for Mental Health Services convened a meeting to better describe Wraparound as one of several "promising practices in child mental health." I was not able to attend that meeting, but Ira did, and I was asked to write part of the report. One of the major issues which emerged at that meeting was that, by its nature, Wraparound is almost impossible to define. The only way to truly define it is by defining the basic elements and accepting the premise that, if one kept to those elements, what ever was being done would be Wraparound.

Since the 1998 meeting, things have evolved to where some of the leaders in Wraparound, in conjunction with the Research and Training Center at

Portland State University in Oregon, have been working to develop a measure of Wraparound validity. What this means is they would like to figure out a way to test to see if what someone is doing is really Wraparound or not. The way they are doing this is to come up with a set of elements and ask participants in a "Wraparound process" how that process rates on holding to the elements. This is important, because as more and more people say they are doing Wraparound, it helps to make sure families are getting the real thing. It is also important because, from a research point of view, it helps document that Wraparound works. At the time of the writing of this chapter, there is a consensus group attempting to come to some new, updated consensus on the elements of Wraparound. The group has not finalized this process, but it looks like the "new" elements will look pretty much like the old ones, only with some different names.

Change is inevitable, and my view is that when we started doing individualized services at Kaleidoscope we didn't call them "Wraparound." We just did what made sense and what fit into our service philosophy. Now, some of us call what we do Wraparound. Many other people provide services that are unconditional and strength-based and that look pretty much like Wraparound, but they call it something else. For example, most family preservation programs are based on these elements. In New Zealand, where I have been working for the last six years, they have an early intervention program called Family Start that is based on the same elements, and uses our Kaleidoscope experience as part of its training. New Zealand also has a social service concept called the Family Group Conference, which looks pretty much like a Child and Family Team to me. I suppose that in the future, what we now call "Wraparound" will look different, be called something else, but have the same underlying elements, which are:

- A practice of unconditional care;

- A focus on individual strengths;

- A family-driven, family-strengths-focused process;

- An individualized approach;

- An emphasis on serving families within their communities;

- A commitment to culturally competent care;

- A process that includes planning with Child and Family Teams;

- An emphasis on interagency collaboration;

- A net result of cost-effectiveness; and

- An outcome-driven process.

This is the same list you found in the chapter about Cindy. Ira and I hope we have been able to make these elements come to life for you through the stories we have told and our discussions about them. We hope that you have been impressed, much as we have been, by the strengths of Cindy, Tyrone and Carol, Alex and Shirley, Brenda, Samuel, Ramon, Larry, Marcus, Desmond, Tori, Thomas, James, Andrew, George, Agnes, Rodney, Jessie, Tad, Becky, Patricia and Richard, and Janice and Jimmy. We hope you can better understand how services provided within the elements of Wraparound have been able to make a positive impact on the lives of these individuals and others with a similar degree of trouble. Finally, we hope, whether you are a family member, family friend, community partner, or service-providing individual, that the stories and lessons in this book have helped you in your struggles to make things better for yourself and your children and/or in your ability to help others.

Often, the stories we have presented in this book appear to be simple fixes. We need to remember, however, that the individuals whose stories we have told all had complex lives with major problems along with their strengths. Sometimes the results of Wraparound are magic, and people's lives are completely turned around. This seemed to be the case with Cindy, who, had she not died of AIDS, may well have fulfilled the promise she showed when she moved back to her home in the South. Other times, people who have used Wraparound to help themselves and/or their families, although they fare much better than previously, still have significant problems with which they continued to struggle after their Kaleidoscope Wraparound care ended. Inasmuch as we can, we'd like to try to fill you in on how the individuals whose stories we have told in this book have done since the time Karl worked with them. Unfortunately, we have lost track of some of the young people and their families, especially in the cases of those individuals and families Karl met while doing consultations in other cities.

Samuel: Samuel has used his strengths to move ahead in life and stay out of trouble. He worked for a year in Kaleidoscope's parking lot, got out of the gangs, lives in the community, and has not been incarcerated. He still struggles with alcohol, however. He shows up at Kaleidoscope from time to time. When he sees Karl, he refers to him as "Dad."

Ramon: Ramon continued to be successful after leaving Kaleidoscope. He got his GED and joined the dance troupe his foster parents ran. Although we have lost track of Ramon, we do know that he continued to be successful for more than two years after leaving Kaleidoscope.

Larry: Larry used Kaleidoscope's services well. He capitalized on his high intellect and learned how to live independently. The last we heard he was maintaining an apartment of his own. When the youth we served at Kaleidoscope do well we tend to lose track of them, and this is what happened with Larry.

Marcus: As we related in the story, Marcus has done well in his life, and runs a group home program in which he helps the next generation of youth. Although, as you will remember from the story, Kaleidoscope's unconditional care philosophy helped Marcus after he burned down the office building, he will not accept firesetters in his group home. This demonstrates that the principles of Wraparound can be very difficult for many people to fully integrate into their professional lives.

Brenda: Brenda lives in the community and has been successful in keeping her emotions in check. She has never had another suicide attempt. Unfortunately, she has struggled with life and does not do the best job supporting herself. She got herself on Disability, and the monthly checks came to Kathy, who acted as her fiscal agent for a long time until Karl and Kathy moved out of Chicago, at which time the job of agent was passed on to someone else. We think this is an excellent way for Kaleidoscope's unconditional care concept to be extended well beyond the organization's official service to Brenda.

Alex: Alex was a brilliant success. Kaleidoscope served him for more than three years, during which time he became an apprentice printer. He continues to do well, and is fond of telling Karl that as a printer, he makes more money than most social workers.

Desmond: Unlike the majority of the youth Kaleidoscope worked with, Desmond had graduated from high school and had been a success before he came there. He continued to be successful in Kaleidoscope services, and after he left, he joined the Job Corps. The last we heard from Desmond, he had entered the Armed Forces.

Tori: Tori is one of the individuals who was able to turn her entire life around. She lives in the community, where she is still working as a real estate salesperson. She is currently studying for her real-estate license so that she can become a broker. She still takes no medication.

Thomas: Thomas' story was told to Karl by Terry Cross. We have no follow-up as to what has happened to him since, but our sense is that his problem was superficial and temporary and he has done well.

Tyrone: Tyrone was another success story, but unfortunately, he passed away during the writing of this book. As we mentioned the the story, Tyrone had beaten his addictions and worked as a drug counselor. He had served on Kaleidoscope's Board of Directors and had represented the agency. In spite of his success, Tyrone never did reclaim custody of his children, whom everyone, including Tyrone, agreed were better off having good times with their father while they lived elsewhere.

Andrew and George: One of sad parts of doing Wraparound consultations in other cities is that often, after the consultation, there are no ongoing connections with those children and their families. This is true with both Andrew and George.

Agnes: Agnes, the first person Karl served, continued to let Karl serve her. They put the plan together and it was successful. At one point she helped another parent to discover that Karl and his coworkers could be trusted.

Rodney: Karl described Rodney's story as tragic. One of his issues was firesetting, which Kaleidoscope was comfortable with handling. At one point during the three years that Rodney received services from Kaleidoscope, he was visiting Karl and found a cigarette lighter, which he brought to Karl, saying, "You shouldn't leave dangerous things like this lying around!" The Department of Social Services was less tolerant than Karl, however. DSS removed Rodney from Kaleidoscope's care and sent him to residential treatment in another state, at which point Karl lost track of him.

Jessie: Jessie did move to the apartment upstairs from her old one. She continued successfully with Kaleidoscope, but Karl was not directly involved, and he has few details of where she is now.

Tad: Tad learned to swear in Polish. His team later put together a plan that focused on issues beyond his swearing, and he did much better. He was never again suspended from school or hospitalized. He graduated from high school and is now gainfully employed.

Becky: As we mentioned in the story, Becky did send her list to Karl and got her doll. Her behavior got a lot better and she graduated from high school and ended up getting a job. We do not think that she ever called Karl's friend about her medical condition. Unfortunately, she has had continued trouble with her medical condition, and the last we heard she was in one of her periodic hospitalizations.

references

Burns, B.J., & Goldman, S.K. (1999). Promising practices in wraparound for children with serious emotional disturbance and their families. *Systems of care: Promising Practices in Children's Mental Health, 1998 series, Vol. IV.* Washington D.C.: Center for Effective Collaboration and Practice, American Institutes for Research.

Community Partnership Group (1995). *Wraparound training manual.* Unpublished document.

Dennis K. W., & Dennis, K. (2003). *Meeting children's and families' needs through the use of child and family teams.* Unpublished training materials.

Kaleidoscope (1992). Principles of local system development for children and adolescents with serious emotional disturbances. Chicago: Author. (Available from Kaleidoscope at 1279 N. Milwaukee Avenue, Chicago, IL, 68990).

New Freedom Commission on Mental Health. (2003). *Achieving the promise: Transforming mental health care in America—Final report.* (DHHS Pub. No. SMA-03-3832). Rockville, MD: Substance Abuse and Mental Health Services Administration. Accessed 12/8/2005 from www.mentalhealthcommission.gov.

For Further Reading

Burchard, J.D., & Burchard, S.N. (1993). *One kid at a time: Evaluative case studies and description of the Alaska youth initiative demonstration project.* Washington, DC: Georgetown University Child Development Center, National Technical Assistance Center for Child Mental Health.

Cross, T.L., Bazron, B.J., Dennis, K.W., & Isaacs, M.R. (1989). *Toward a culturally competent system of care.* Washington, DC: Georgetown University Child Development Center, National Technical Assistance Center for Child Mental Health.

Katz-Leavy, J., Lourie, I., Stroul, B. & Zeigler-Dendy, C. (1992). *Individualized services in a system of care*. Washington, DC: Georgetown University Child Development Center, National Technical Assistance Center for Child Mental Health.

Lourie, I., Howe, S., & Roebuck, L. (1996). *Systematic approaches to mental health care in the private sector for children, adolescents, and their families: Managed care organizations and service providers*. Washington, DC: Georgetown University Child Development Center, National Technical Assistance Center for Child Mental Health.

about the authors

Karl W. Dennis is one of the country's pioneers and leading experts in providing community-based care for the "hardest-to-serve" children and families through Wraparound services, therapeutic foster care, pediatric AIDS care, independent living, and long-term intensive family preservation services. He was the Executive Director of the Chicago-area agency Kaleidoscope for 27 years until his retirement in 2002. Under his direction, Kaleidoscope became nationally recognized as one of the top five child-serving agencies in the country. Currently, Karl is the President of Karl W. Dennis & Associates, which has provided long-term training and consultation on Wraparound initiatives and services, child welfare, and related issues in all 50 states and the District of Columbia, the U.S. Virgin Islands, Canada, China, Guam, and New Zealand. Karl also currently chairs the Children's Committee of the National Mental Health Association. Among other honors, he has received the Lifetime Achievement Award from the International Conference on Wraparound Services; the President's 1000 Points of Light Award; Texas Hero Award for service to the children and families of Texas; The Karl Dennis Annual Award for Unconditional Care, created by the Federation of Families for Children's Mental Health; the Annie E. Casey Foundation National Honors Award; The National Award for Advocacy on Behalf of Children and Families from the American Association of Community Psychiatrists; The Marion Langer Award from the American Orthopsychiatric Association; and the Making a Difference

Award from the Federation of Families for Children's Mental Health. He has also been inducted into both the National Basketball Hall of Fame as a member of the DuSable Panthers High School Team. Karl and his wife, Kathy, currently live in Michigan City, IN.

Ira S. Lourie, MD, a child psychiatrist, is currently a partner in the Human Service Collaborative, which provides consultation, technical assistance, and training in human service policy and service system development. He is also Medical Director of AWARE, an agency for troubled children in Anaconda, Montana; and psychiatric consultant for two other agencies that provide community-based services in Maryland, Pressely Ridge Maryland and the Catholic Charities Villa Maria Consortium. From 1973 to 1991, Ira worked at the National Institute of Mental Health (NIMH) where he was instrumental in the development and administration of the Child and Adolescent Service System Program (CASSP). Prior to his work on CASSP, he focused on the development of services for abused and neglected adolescents. He is assistant clinical professor of Child Psychiatry at the Georgetown University School of Medicine and a past member of the Task Force on Systems of Care for Seriously Emotionally Disturbed Children of the American Academy of Child and Adolescent Psychiatry. Dr. Lourie is a Past President of the American Orthopsychiatric Association. He is a former member of the Board of Directors of the Federation of Families for Child Mental Health and of the Board of Trustees for the Council on Accreditation. Among the many honors he has received are the Lifetime Achievement Award from the International Conference on Wraparound Services, the Outstanding Service Medal from the U.S. Public Health Service for his pioneering work on behalf of abused and neglected adolescents, the Gwen Iding Lectureship from the Research and Training Center for Children's Mental Health at the University of South Florida, the Making a Difference Award from the Federation of Families for Child Mental Health, and the Tipper Gore "Remember the Children Award" from the National Mental Health Association. He and his wife, Carrol, currently live in Hagerstown, Maryland.